DAUGHTER OF THE LAND

To Vicky ~

with my best wishes

to a new neighbor!

Betsy

June 2022

DAUGHTER OF THE LAND

Growing Up in the Citrus Capital of the World

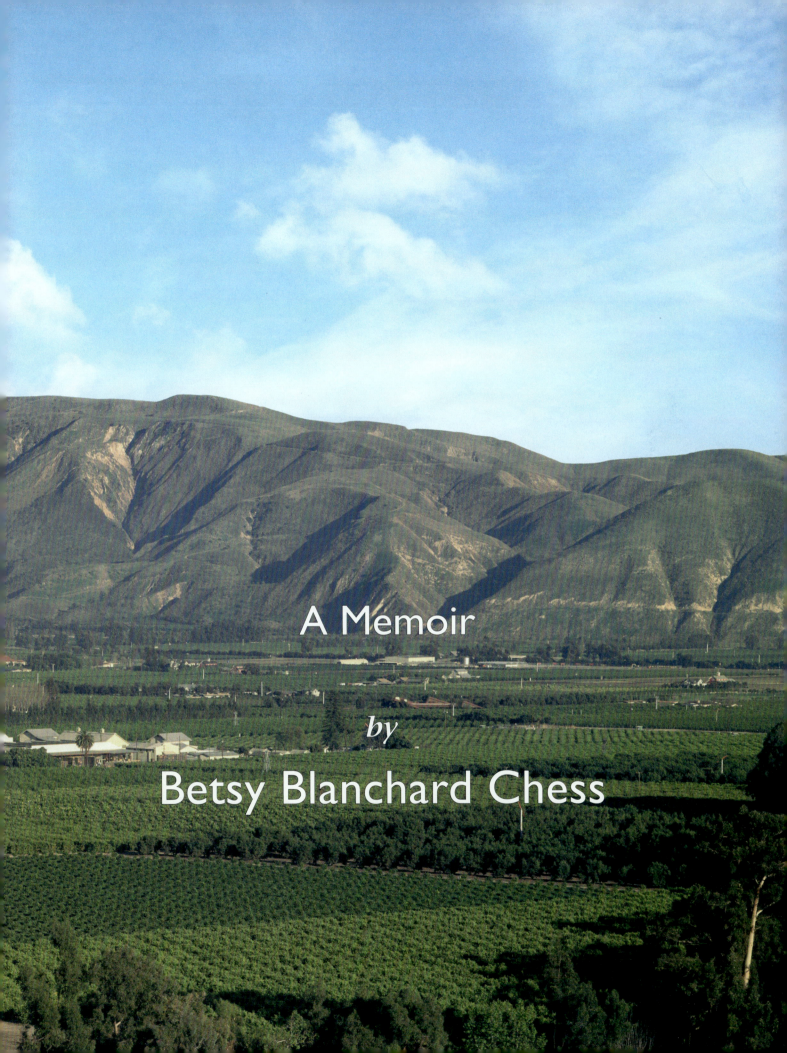

A Memoir

by

Betsy Blanchard Chess

Daughter of the Land: *Growing Up in the Citrus Capital of the World*: A Memoir

First edition—2021

Manufactured in the United States of America.

ISBN 978-0-578-84863-1 (cloth)

LCCN 2021903187

For further information see:
http://BetsyChessBooks.com/

FRONT COVER AND TITLE PAGE: *Photo by John Blanchard. Courtesy Limoneira Company.*

ENDSHEETS: *Colorized lithograph of Blanchard & Bradley orange orchard taken from Oakland publisher Thompson & West's* History of Santa Barbara & Ventura Counties, *published in 1883.*

LAYOUT AND DESIGN: Charles Nelson Johnson: **HISTORY***by***DESIGN**

Acknowledgments

SO MANY PEOPLE HELPED ME CREATE this book; some in very tangible ways and others by means of a suggestion or perhaps pointing me to another source of information or inspiration.

My thanks first to my brother, John Blanchard, who has walked every step of this family path with me, and to my daughter, Devon and her husband Vince Cichoski, who with their new daughter, Eliza Joy, will walk that path long after I have gone. I so wish my brother Jim was still here to read the book, but his daughters and their girls will do so. I appreciate as well, good friends Judy Warner, Joni and Bob Egbert, and Ron Thompson who gallantly read the first drafts.

This book would not have come about without the superb editing and design skills of Charles Johnson. We found we made a good team–he is a researcher and California historian extraordinaire who made sure my evolving manuscript was both factual as well as a good read. Charles and I both tip our hats to Cherie Brant, who is the best proof reader in the known world. Thanks also to Henry Dubroff, founder and publisher of the *Pacific Coast Business Times*, whose cogent suggestions along the way always prompted me to think about my emerging story in new ways. Plus he agreed to write the book's foreword.

Many thanks go to John Chamberlain, former vice president of marketing at Limoneira, who offered suggestions and encouragement and directed me to designer Kit Hinrics in San Francisco from whom I received my first primer in book design and publishing. Thanks also go to the four readers who reviewed the (almost) final manuscript: Ventura County historians Judy Triem and Mitch Stone; Tim Gallagher, co-owner 20/20 Network and former editor and publisher of the *Ventura County Star*; and author and raconteur, the irrepressible, Ivor Davis.

Thanks to Craig Held, who shared his Santa Paula library and Blanchard family files; to John Nichols for help both finding photos and taking them; to cousins Weston Blanchard Richardson and J. Wyatt Merriman, the first for passing along the Thacher letter and the latter for a photograph of his grandmother, "Cousin E" and Kelly; to Alfonso Guilin for his insight and knowledge of agricultural labor relations; to John Krist, CEO of the Farm Bureau of Ventura County, whose thorough grasp of farming history of the county was invaluable; to John Orr for sharing his memories of a magical summer in Israel in 1968; to the research staff of the Huntington Library for sending me a copy of Nathan Weston Blanchard's journal; and equally to Deya Terrafranca, research library and archives director at the Museum of Ventura County, for providing me access to the Blanchard Collection housed there, and to Renee Tallent, museum collections manager, who helped me decipher the handwriting of 150-year-old family letters; thanks to Limoneira CEO Harold Edwards for his comments on my final draft and for his help making sure the Limoneira story was accurate.

And finally, I must thank the Blanchard Community Library. I attended an event there celebrating 110 years of operation. The event was at the end of February 2020, just two weeks before the Covid-19 lockdown. As my brother John and I recounted our memories to the guests, I realized it was time to stop procrastinating and write the family history I had been incubating for so long. And who would have thought the lockdown would provide further impetus—The Perfect Pandemic Project!

Foreword

by Henry Dubroff

When Betsy Chess asked me to take a look at an early draft of her personal memoir, she described it as a way to tell her family's story so that future generations might understand how the Blanchard family had come to be part of the fabric of Santa Paula.

As I began to read the early drafts and as the extraordinary events of 2020 unfolded, it occurred to me that *Daughter of the Land* might be a richer text by placing her personal history in the context of larger developments. For anyone but a gifted story teller this might have been a daunting task. But Betsy knows how to manage a complex narrative and she has natural good judgement, so this personal history also tells the story of changes that have taken place in the culture of California's Central Coast during nearly a century and a half.

It should be said that I've known Betsy and her family for many years. Limoneira, the company that her great-grandfather co-founded in 1893, has been the subject of much reporting in *Pacific Coast Business Times*, the business journal I founded in 2000. I'm honored that she quoted from a special publication we designed for the 125th anniversary of Limoneira. I was delighted when the board elected her to its board of directors, a move toward gender diversity that was probably long overdue.

What makes *Daughter of the Land* special, in my view, is that it takes the opportunity to look back at history to speak about our time. Beginning with a serious illness she suffered at age nine—we begin to understand how life was before there was a vaccine for polio and we perhaps learn a bit about what the COVID-19 survivors are facing. We learn more about the women who created the civic culture of Santa Paula and fostered it patiently through the floods, freezes, droughts and more recently fires, that disrupt an idyllic place from time to time.

We get a glimpse into the early years of a young woman growing up at a prosperous time in a family of substance and heritage. But Betsy's gift is to look back not with nostalgia but with a growing awareness of bigger issues like farm labor, race relations, the role of women and a company's social responsibilities. She has performed a valuable service by looking at these issues from the perspective of the twenty-first century.

Betsy Chess has had a life well lived. She's been more successful than she suggests and she's impacted the lives of thousands. That alone would be enough. But *Daughter of the Land* does something else. It places her life in the context of her family's past and our extraordinarily disrupted present in her unique and confident voice.

TABLE OF CONTENTS

"Father loved the wonder of this country; he would stand on the porch gazing across to Mupu Mountain—South Mountain, and exclaim, 'This is a beautiful valley—a beautiful valley!' I looked at it thinking it was horrid, for all I saw was sagebrush, cactus and oak trees, and I could distinguish nothing lovely about it. I have often wished since that I might see with fresh eyes, for now I know how truly beautiful it is."

Sarah Eliot Blanchard, age ninety-three,
reminiscing about her father,
Nathan Weston Blanchard

Introduction

I WAS BORN TO A TIME AND TO A WAY OF LIFE that no longer exists, but to a place that still has surprising relevance in twenty-first century Southern California—the enduring little city of Santa Paula, California. Situated in the lovely Santa Clara Valley, Santa Paula was the cradle of both the California citrus and oil industries.

Santa Paula was founded in 1873 by my great-grandfather, Nathan Weston Blanchard (NWB),[1] who had come from Maine to make his fortune in the California gold fields two decades earlier. He never found gold, but when he relocated south to the fertile and climate-favored Santa Clara Valley, he made a fortune in a different kind of gold—oranges and lemons.

Great-grandfather planted 100 acres of citrus in 1874, but it took the orchard fourteen years before it came into bearing. By 1891 however, he was shipping thousands of pounds of fruit to the East Coast where eating a fresh orange in December was considered a marvel.

In 1893, NWB and Wallace Libbey Hardison, co-founder of the Union Oil Company, created the Limoneira Company.[2] At a time when the average lemon ranch in the region ranged from one to fifteen acres, in 1904 the Limoneira Company farmed 400 acres of lemons, oranges and walnuts, and by 1907 had increased its acreage to 2,490 acres with accompanying water rights.

In 1911, the *Santa Paula Chronicle* proclaimed Limoneira to be "The World's Largest Citrus Ranch," and Santa Paula to be "The Citrus Capital of the World." By 1922, one in every eight lemons consumed in the United States came from Ventura County, most from Limoneira.[3]

Nathan Blanchard and his wife, Ann Elizabeth Hobbs, were central to Santa Paula and the region's social and cultural life, supporting the Congregational and Methodist churches, establishing the Santa Paula Academy (soon to become Santa Paula High School), helping to found Pomona College, and, in 1910, giving the city a fine library, the Dean

---

[1] Great-grandfather was referred to by his initials. Since there is now an NWB V, this is a very useful shorthand.

[2] The name Limoneira was chosen by NWB and is Portuguese for "lemon tree." I believe he was fascinated by the language that he heard spoken by the Basque sheepherders of the area who came each year to the Blanchard Ranch for sheep shearing. The name of my family home, *Los Limoneiros*, was also of Portuguese derivation.

[3] Margo McBane, "Whitening a California Citrus Company Town: Racial Segregation Practices at the Limoneira Company and Santa Paula, 1893-1919." (2010)

Hobbs Blanchard Memorial Library, named for their beloved first-born son, who had died in 1871.

When great-grandfather, often referred to as the "Father of Santa Paula," died in 1917, the city closed from 11:00 a.m-1:00 p.m. in honor of, "…a long life nobly lived."[4]

This was the background I was born into, the privileged daughter of a proud pioneer family. The Blanchard family of my youth lived on a hill above the northwestern part of the city in a compound consisting of three homes, gardens, stables, and various other structures, including a red brick dormitory and office built in the last decade of the nineteenth century. My great aunt, Sarah Eliot Blanchard, was not only the family matriarch, but also an iconic and revered link to the town's earliest days. We were the epitome of that timeworn phrase, "big fish in a small pond."

Not that we didn't live up to the challenge. My parents, Eliot McClelland Blanchard and Elizabeth Irene Munger, actively supported the life and economy of Santa Paula and the county. Mom was on Santa Paula Elementary and High School boards for seventeen years and was, among many, many other things, the first woman to be foreperson of the Ventura County Grand Jury. Dad, a Stanford-educated lawyer, was a life-long farm manager, entrepreneur and active member of the local Rotary Club and Masonic Temple, as well as myriad industry boards. I was almost pre-destined to follow their example of community engagement.

Have you ever looked at the usually stern and unsmiling portraits of your ancestors? At some point you realize they weren't always old, and might begin to wonder about their early lives and times. If you are lucky, as I have been, you have access to source materials from those early days, and the time and the tools to weave together their stories.

That's what I've been doing during these long days of unprecedented isolation and social distancing occasioned by the Covid-19 pandemic. I've come to realize that what I have discovered isn't just a family story, but also the story of a burgeoning western community, with all the twists and turns, peaks and valleys such a history involves.

The following narrative is part memoir, part social history, part agricultural history, especially that of the Limoneira Company, and part pledge to great-aunt Sarah,[5] that I shall never take the beauty of this place for granted.

Betsy Blanchard Chess
February 2021, in the time of Covid-19

_____

[5] Although Sarah was my great aunt, I shall refer to her as Aunt Sarah going forward.

Aunt Sarah as I knew her in 1957 as I was recovering from a possible bout with polio. Her hands were never idle and I never remember her without that gentle smile.

_____

[4] Dean Hobbs Blanchard, *Of California's First Citrus Empire: A Rainbow Arches from Maine to Ventura County* (1983), 188.

Childhood in the Citrus Capital of the World

El Naranjal, or "place of the orange," pictured here in 1965, went through many iterations before becoming the gracious home of Sarah Blanchard that I knew.

IN 1959, WHEN I WAS ELEVEN years old, the 160-acre Blanchard Ranch on the western edge of Santa Paula was sold and subdivided. My great aunt and grand dame of the family, Sarah Eliot Blanchard, lived in her majestic old home, *El Naranjal* (place of the orange), on about ten acres adjacent to the former ranch property.

The grounds of *El Naranjal* were wonderful; full of specimen trees, flower gardens, green houses, a tennis court, corrals and stables. The southern edge of the property was marked by huge eucalyptus trees, thick and shaggy, which happily shed leaves and pods over the newly laid streets. In 1961, the city of Santa Paula asked that she cut down some of the worst offenders.

My father and I stood with Aunt Sarah as the messy giants came down. As we watched, she turned to me and said, "I was here when we planted those trees."

Even then I knew the idea of comparing one's life to the life of a tree was stunning. The thought resonated deep within me and set me on my path as a student and life-long lover of history.

Aunt Sarah had great influence in our family. She was smart, funny, well-traveled and the last family connection to the time of Santa Paula's founding. She once said the reason she never married was because her sister, Eunice, married the only available bachelor in town.

Sarah Blanchard, age 36, in 1904. Sarah was to say, with a twinkle in her eye, that the reason she never married was because Eunice married the only available bachelor in town.

Eunice Blanchard at the age of 33 just before her marriage to Dr. Arthur Kelsey.

She also had an important, if much more subtle influence on me. In 1957, when I was nine years old, the Salk vaccine against polio was developed and given to school children across the country, myself and my classmates at Barbara Webster School among them. Towards the end of that year about Christmas time, I developed terrible cramps in my legs.

The osteopath put this down to "growing pains," but by the time my parents had a big Christmas party a day or two later, I was in bed sick. Dr. Artemus Strong, pioneer Santa Clara Valley physician and the man who had delivered me, stuck his head into my room to check on me. I was stark-raving delirious with fever. He grabbed me by the arm and dragged me into the bathroom where he thrust me under a cold shower.

Polio was still very much on people's minds even with the advent of the new vaccine, and my symptoms—leg cramps and high fever—were alarming. I spent the next two weeks in isolation at the old Foster Hospital, predecessor of Community Memorial, in Ventura. I remember that experience vaguely—all alone except for my white Breyer plastic horse, Silver, and a much-loved blue stuffed horse named Charger. Strange adults in white came and went. What was I suffering from? Was it polio; a reaction to the new vaccine; a case of polio arrested by the vaccine? Or was it meningitis, another possibility as my spine was stiff and inflexible?

A spinal tap would have answered the questions definitively, but it was a risky procedure for a child and one of last resort. Fortunately, I began to recover, so to this day the mystery illness was never diagnosed.

I don't remember feeling frightened. I think at nine I was oblivious to the fears that swirled around me. At any rate, I was sent home to convalesce. Weak and emaciated, I spent the next six weeks in bed. Enter Aunt Sarah. Several times a week she would arrive, arms full of books, and read to me. I still have my favorite of those books, a gorgeously illustrated copy of Nathaniel Hawthorne's *A Wonder Book and Tanglewood Tales*. I was introduced to the world of Greek mythology; a world of gods and goddesses, heroes and villains, a subject I love to this day. Years later when I took a course on mythology at USC, I realized the myths I had learned about were a very much sanitized version of the X-rated lives of the Greek, Roman and Norse gods.

Another hero to me during that time was Paul Keith, father of my best friend, Dennis, and manager of the Santa Paula branch of Bank of America. Paul came to visit one day with a bag full of pennies, a magnifying glass, a reference book, and display books full of indented spots for specially identified pennies. Was the penny minted in Sacramento or Denver? Was it a rare penny from a limited run? I spent many an otherwise boring hour searching through my penny hoard. What a thoughtful gift to give to a bedbound child.

One day, a couple of weeks into my convalescence, my mom came into my room with an envelope full of letters from my classmates. I excitedly dived in. It was wonderful to hear from my friends

Me holding Charger, with my brother Jim in 1954. In 1957 blue stuffed Charger was to be my only companion as I spent two weeks in isolation in Foster Hospital for fear I had polio.

until I read a letter that said, "Is it true? Did you have polio?" I remember shrieking in horror. I truly did not realize how sick I had been.

Many times during the early days of my illness, doctors would ask me to touch my chin to my chest—a possible sign of meningitis if one couldn't do that. I had no idea this was diagnostic. When I returned to my fourth-grade class in the spring, I led a PE activity. I asked my class to circle 'round and touch their chins to their chests. I guess I just thought it was some kind of fitness test.

Today, I often think back to that time when the advent of a vaccine was embraced as a miracle of science. How different now when a vocal minority rebels against mandatory childhood vaccinations to prevent measles, mumps and rubella, and some are prepared to continue this resistance if a vaccine for Covid-19 becomes mandatory.

In the time before the polio vaccine, thousands were killed, crippled or relegated to life in an iron lung. In 1952, at the height of the polio epidemic in the United States, 57,628 cases were reported; 3,145 people died and more than 20,000 were left with mild to disabling paralysis.

Left: My mother, Elizabeth Munger Blanchard, and brothers John and Jim standing in front of our family home *Los Limoneiros* before it was remodeled in 1948, the year I was born.

Below: John, Betsy and Jim coming down the steps of our wonderful old Santa Paula home on Easter 1952.
Photo: Robert Dana Teague.

The scourges of the past—small pox, diphtheria, scarlet fever, whooping cough, polio and so many other diseases, were virtually eliminated by the creation of a vaccine. We forget these lessons at our peril.

Likewise, I find eerie parallels between the current resistance to wearing masks, and the similar resistance 100 years ago at the time of the Spanish Flu pandemic of 1918. As the old song says, "When will we ever learn?"

Meanwhile, fully recovered from my bout with the mystery illness, I returned to a life on the ranch in Santa Paula that was magical. Our home was just up the hill from Aunt Sarah's. It, too, had a name—*Los Limoneiros* (roughly, "lemon lands"), a big Craftsman home built in 1912 by Nathan, Sr. and his wife as a gift to my paternal grandparents, Nathan Weston Blanchard, Jr. and Josephine Esther Blanchard (Grandma Tiny). My parents bought it in 1946 after dad returned from the war. Famed local architect Roy Wilson remodeled the home into a residence that was both elegant and functional. Built around a central courtyard that eventually featured a swimming pool, my mom called it a "woman killer" because you could only access the two wings of the house via a central hallway. The laundry room, for instance, was on one side of the house, but the bedroom wing was on the other so laundry day meant ferrying dirty clothes, sheets, towels, etc. across that hall to wash, and then hauling everything back again when clean. This was especially inconvenient if you wanted a drink of water in the middle of the night or craved a midnight snack. I remember the lawn in the central courtyard because each morning as I trekked from my room to the kitchen down that hallway, I would peek out the windows hoping that during the night a horse might have been delivered. I was the youngest of three children. My brother Jim was seven years older, and as such rather distant and godlike. John was five years older, but wonderfully fun and a great pal. Well, most of the time. He loved to tease me. He would say, "Boo, (my childhood nickname) you want to go buy a horse?" Like an eager puppy, I practically wiggled in anticipation.

"You go down to the garage and get in the car, I'll bring mom down in a minute." Down to the garage I would go and into the car to wait…and wait. Needless to say, mom never came. I can't tell you the number of times I fell for that trick.

"Oh, if only I were older!" I wistfully stare out the window at the pool party given in honor of cousin Robin Blanchard who had just graduated from the Thacher School in 1958. *Photo: Walt Dibblee.*

The three of us playing in the coach barn, 1952. *Photo: Robert Dana Teague.*

Life on the ranch was filled with adventure and a wonderful place to let childhood imaginations flourish. Jim and John, and cousins Amy and Nathan, established the Dare Devil Club, initiation to join was to cross a narrow beam over a cement floor twenty feet below.

My younger friends and I played RinTinTin, a much safer game, in the tack room of the old coach barn. Cramped and dusty, it was a magical cave filled with saddles, bridles and other tack, some currently used, but most from a bygone era. We didn't care. Our gang, usually consisting of Dennis and Sharon Keith and Meredith Hopkins, would clamber up onto the saddles and ride away! My ancient German Shorthaired Pointer, Jill, filled in for Rinny, and that worked just fine. On the days we were Robin Hood and his band of Merry Men,

Brothers John and Jim at Christmas 1945 with Smokey, the first of our mother's many longhaired cats. *Photo: Robert Dana Teague.*

we left Fort Apache and took our games to a giant pepper tree, whose huge, sloping branches and overhead canopy of leaves was the perfect Sherwood Forest.

Animals played a big part of my childhood. Being the only girl with brothers five and seven years older, animals often were my only companions. There were two dogs named Jill, both German Shorthaired Pointers that came from rancher Glen Good. There was Smokey, first in a succession of my mother's beloved longhaired cats. There was a huge flock of chickens that provided eggs for the various branches of the family, and usually a steer or two and lambs that were raised on the ranch by members of nearby Santa Paula High School's Future Farmers of America (FFA).

And there were always horses. Although neither of my parents particularly liked horses, Aunt Sarah was a superb horsewoman and made sure horses were a part of our life. She told the story of the time she and a girl friend put their fathers' saddles on their horses and rode out "astride," instead of the accepted sidesaddle. They rode past a field where a man was working. Seeing them go by, she said he dropped his hoe and gazed in shock.

First in my memory of important horses were Pepper and Sugar. Pepper was a bombproof little strawberry roan that came from the Juaregui Ranch up Wheeler Canyon. One day, when I was about five, I was standing half way in the corral holding tight to the big gate while I chatted with Pepper. Unfortunately, that gate got too heavy and I let it go.

It only took Pepper a moment to make the most of the situation. With a swish of his red tail he was out of the corral and heading across the ranch at

I arrived in 1948, quite the baby princess according to my brothers. At our mother's memorial in 2009, John got a fond chuckle from the congregation when he said, "Jim and I were doing just fine, and then Betsy came along!"

Me in the tack room of the coach barn mounting up for unknown adventures in 1952. *Photo: Robert Dana Teague.*

Betsy, John and Jim on Pepper in 1952, with the mule barn in the background. *Photo: Robert Dana Teague.*

full gallop. I, of course, was in big trouble, only saved when Pepper arrived back at the Juaregui Ranch a few hours later. It was some jailbreak—out across the ranch, right turn at the corner of what is now Santa Paula Street and Foothill Road, west on Foothill to Wheeler Canyon, and right turn up the canyon for the final two-mile sprint. Some homing device that horse had—a trek of more than ten miles.

Pepper's companion was Sugar, a flashy little liver chestnut mare with a perfect white sugar beet blaze down her face. Sugar was on loan to my brother Jim from George Harding, who ran the hardware store in town. She was as hot as she was pretty, and Jim was the only one who could handle her. I held both of them in awe.

One day, when I was in kindergarten, Jim took me riding with him. I was in heaven until we cantered across Cemetery Road on the western border of the ranch and hopped over a little ditch on the other side. Jim and Sugar jumped it beautifully, but I fell off Pepper in mid leap and landed in the middle of the ditch with a broken arm.

Jim came galloping back and looked at me in horror. All he could think about was how mad mom was going to be. He looked down at me as I sat blubbering at the bottom of the ditch clutching my arm and said, "Wasn't that fun?" Good try, Jim. My arm was badly broken and I'm sure there was hell to pay.

Next in my long line of equines was Sweetie Pie, a bay pony that belonged to my cousin Amy, who lived with us during her high school years

The family posse. L to R: Amy on Sweetie Pie, John on Pepper with me as eager groom, Jim on Buck overseen by Elizabeth.

after the death of her mother, Barbara. Amy was the most accomplished horsewoman in the family,

On beautiful Red Lauro, Big Red, in 1963. The photo was to be part of an article for *Teen Magazine*. It was due to come out in November of 1963, but that issue was completely changed due to the assassination of President Kennedy, so it never appeared.

a skill she parlayed into a professional career. Sweetie Pie loved Amy—me, not so much. She tolerated me for a couple of years until the arrival of Goldie, a cute little palomino mare with a nasty temper—turn your back and she'd take a chunk out of you.

My luck finally changed when I was twelve and my parents bought me a gorgeous chestnut Quarter Horse named Red Lauro. Big Red was a source of quite the object lesson. I only had him a few months

I so remember Aunt Sarah taking this photo of Goldie and me in 1958. She stood a few feet away staring intently into her big box camera. The sun was in my eyes and I thought she was taking forever!

when in the midst of play, he kicked out and caught me in the face. Afraid my parents would take him away, I told them I had happened on a game of father-son football and had been hit in the face by an errant ball. Amazingly, mom and dad chose to believe me, but when I was bragging about my cover up at school, Mr. Lock, the seventh grade teacher we had at Isbell and whom we all adored, happened to hear. He paused as he walked by and said to me, "I would have thought better of you." My friends and I were stunned—a first lesson in being an accountable adult had been delivered.

Big Red remained in the family for more than twenty years, ending his final days with my cousin, Ann Munger.

In later years I turned from riding Western style to riding big hunters and jumpers. From 1970-2018, I was accompanied by Breeze, Ticker Tape, Pele, Page, Riker, Elliot Ness, Smoke and Mirrors, Obermie, Kramer and Timeless. Whether it was blue ribbons or broken bones, I loved them all and enjoyed every minute.

RIGHT: Back surgery among other things took me off horses from 1985 to 2003. Here I am on Elliot Ness at the Santa Barbara "Turkey Show" in 2005.

ABOVE: Alaric (Kramer) and I in 2015 placing in the top five in the Hunter Derby at Flintridge Riding Club.

LEFT: The Staben Ranch in Santa Paula was a popular horse show venue. I love this photo of me on Over the Counter (Breeze), taken in 1974, because of the perfect balance of both horse and rider and the beautiful country background.

RIGHT: Another shot taken at Flintridge Riding Club in 2010 of a horsemanship final on Smoke and Mirrors (Smokey).

LEFT: I love the explosive power this photo captures. It was taken in 2007 at Pebble Beach on Elliot Ness. The fluffy boots on the horse's front legs mean that it was an equitation class, i.e. the form of the rider was being judged, not that of the horse.

The Eatons' Ranch

THERE WAS A SPECIAL PLACE for the Blanchard family where everyone rode, regardless of whether it was a favorite activity or not. This was the Eatons' Ranch in Wolf, Wyoming, just outside of Sheridan. Aunt Sarah first discovered it in the early 1920s when she and my grandparents explored Glacier National Park, and we have been vacationing there for the last 100 years.

Aunt Sarah, second from right, at Eatons' Ranch in 1923. Note the proper "English" attire of the ladies; no Wild West look for them!

The Nathan Weston Blanchard, Jr. family at Eatons' in 1929. L to R: Dean, Eliot, Weston, Grandma Tiny and NWB, Jr. I love my father, Eliot's, giant hat and Dean's, always the outlier, saddle shoes!

Eatons' Ranch is the oldest dude ranch in the United States. It was founded as a horse and cattle ranch in 1879 by three brothers—Howard, Willis and Alden, in Medora, North Dakota. Friends from the East Coast began to visit them and some of the early guests stayed for months at a time. Finally, one of the guests, or "dudes" as the Eatons called them, recognized the expense and encouraged them to charge for room and board. Thus the dude ranch industry was born.[6]

In 1904, in order to provide more suitable riding terrain for their guests, the Eatons moved to the present location on Wolf Creek near Sheridan, located on 7,000 acres of rolling grass land beneath the shadow of the Big Horn Mountains. Dotted with pines and cotton woods that line the edges of the streams that come down from the mountains, the ranch is home to several hundred head of cattle as well as deer, antelope, elk, eagles and bears.

I have visited the ranch with my parents, and later with my own family, more than a dozen times—and

[6] David R. Stoeklin and Carrie Lightner, *Dude Ranches of the American West* (2004).

it never seems to change. When I look at the pictures of Aunt Sarah in 1923, and my father and his family in 1929, I realize that in fact, it has changed very little from that time either.

One of the mainstays of a visit to Eatons' is the Dude/Wrangler baseball game played every Sunday throughout the summer. The Wranglers usually won, after all, their team played every week. But on a July Sunday in 1952, my first trip to the ranch, they met their match: my dad, Eliot Blanchard, high school star; Grampa John Munger, minor league prospect had not his mother objected to playing professional baseball on Sundays; and my uncle, Dr. John Roger Munger, who went to Stanford on a full-ride baseball scholarship. The game was epic—home runs, close calls at every base and a cheering crowd made up of dudes, ranch staff and half the population of Sheridan, who drove over for the occasion and watched the Dudes take down the Wranglers!

I remember losing my first tooth at Eatons' that summer of 1952, and the tooth fairy exchanged it for a silver dollar. Unfortunately that dollar didn't

Devon in 1984. Each guest, or dude, is assigned a horse, which is hers to ride for duration of their stay. Devon seems pretty happy with her choice.

last long. At the airport on the way home with my grandparents, Grampa John realized he didn't have any change to tip the porter. He turned to me imploringly—and there went that silver dollar. To a good cause, I guess, but I hated to give it up.

Eatons' was also the source of a wonderful family love story. In the mid-1940s, my father's cousin, Elizabeth Kelsey Merriman, was divorced—a real social shocker at that time. The family sent Cousin E, as I knew her, to Palm Springs to recover from the experience. The beautiful Elizabeth attracted the attention of her tennis coach, so the family whisked her back to Santa Paula. Next she went skiing at Yosemite, but her skiing instructor was equally smitten.

Finally, the family shipped her off to Eatons' thinking surely she would be safe there. Fate laughed. She met one of the wranglers, the dashing Maurice Stephen (Kelly) Howie from South Dakota. They fell in love, married and lived happily ever after.

Devon, Betsy and Dick in 1990. I remember my horse was called Alibi, and I was able to ride him each of the next three years that we visited Eatons'.

We all loved Cousin Kelly—wrangler, horse rancher, steer roper, polo player, and golfer (in cowboy boots with golf studs). He became a Ventura County favorite when he joined the Rancheros Visitadores, a group of riders who meet each year to ride, play and perhaps drink a bit.

This beautiful portrait of Elizabeth Blanchard Kelsey, or Cousin E., shows why she was so eagerly sought after.

Kelly and Elizabeth Howie in 1982. Theirs is a love story recounted at Eatons' to this day.

Dick's grandchildren joined us for a wonderful stay at the ranch in 2009. L to R: Juliana Tabler, Phoebe Chess, Connor Chess, Bennett Chess, Catie Chess and Cynthia Tabler.

The Eatons' Ranch love stories continue—Devon and Vince Cichoski in 2018.

Santa Paula in the 1950s-1960s

LIFE DURING MY PRE-TEEN YEARS was idyllic. Tree-lined streets, good, safe schools and neighborhoods, Santa Paula was a great place to grow up in the 'fifties. And there was something special about being a pre-teen to early-teen girl—my friends and I were bold and fearless.

The bell for recess or lunch would ring at Isbell School and we seventh and eighth graders would charge outside to play—tetherball, baseball, and basketball—whatever was in season. We played hard against each other and against the boys, and we played to win.

One time my dad had gone to a birthday party for the manager of the Blue Goose packing house in Santa Paula. As a gag, the manager was given a large goose. Dad ended up bringing it home because there was a big, nearly empty reservoir on the ranch and he thought the goose could go into it until someone figured out what to do with it.

My best friend, Donna Crouch, and I had a great idea. We were on the Santa Paula High School swim team, and we thought it would be a great joke if we took the goose down to the high school pool, where it would be paddling as the team came to practice.

The goose had other ideas. Have you ever tried to capture an unhappy goose? We chased after it; we split up and tried to flank it. No go. The goose

Another photo taken for the cancelled November 1963 *Teen Magazine* article. It is special because it shows such lovely interaction between best friends—myself and Donna Crouch (Linderos). Donna went into a career in city government and was Ventura city manager from 2005-2013.

finally flew above the two of us and, neck stretched out like an angry snake and wings folded in attack mode, it dive bombed, hissing malevolently as it came at us like a super-charged kamikaze.

Hmmm, back to the drawing board. I would have called it a day, but not Donna. It was her idea to use one of dad's old navy blankets and with each of us holding a side, we rushed the goose and dropped the blanket over it. Success! We gathered up the captive critter and marched off towards the pool about a half-mile away. I remember it was no easy task as the bird weighed a good twenty pounds and still wasn't into the plan.

Fortunately, as it turned out, we met the high school superintendent, Buck Buchan, as we made

On Big Red in front of the coach barn. I'm sure I took for granted the beauty and uniqueness of the Queen Anne–style barn I was in and out of almost every day of my young life. This was taken in 1963.

father's K-rations left over from the war. Packaged meats, even ancient candy bars weren't of much interest, but the three-packs of cigarettes sure were. The ranch was the perfect place for illicit experimentation and we smoked at least a dozen of those vile things in the old coach barn. None of us ever became smokers so I guess we learned a lesson courtesy of the U.S. Army.

But one of my favorite memories was when Donna and I led poor Goldie up the three flights of cement stairs in front of her house. I'm sure there was a good reason, but I have no idea what it was. Miraculously, we got the little mare to the top without breaking one of her legs. The stairs didn't fare so well. Later that evening mom got a call from Donna's dad, Bill, who said the horse's steel-shod hooves had chipped several steps.

our way down the hill to the pool. What a sight we must have been—two 13-year-olds struggling to hold something under a blanket from which protruded a pair of goose legs.

"Girls," he asked sternly, "What are you doing?" We happily explained our scheme because we thought it was a really terrific idea. To our surprise, he did not share our enthusiasm and ordered us to return the goose to the reservoir.

A short time later he called mom, who was on the high school board and said, "Elizabeth, do you know what would have happened if those girls had put that animal in the pool?" Well, evidently health laws would have required the pool be drained, cleaned and refilled before it could be used again.

All these years later I still laugh. What happened to the goose, you ask? I think it went home with Justo, the ranch foreman, and became Thanksgiving dinner.

Another incident I remember was when Vicky Tubbs, another great friend along with Donna and Sylvia McNutt, found, of all things, some of her

My version of this carefree childhood continued from Isbell School to Santa Paula High School, where several influential teachers like the previously mentioned Mr. Lock and band teacher Ed Roina shaped so many of us. I remember our eighth grade graduation dance, with Mr. Roina as the master of ceremonies. He took great glee in embarrassing us, boys and girls alike, as we embarked on our tentative first dating relationships.

Although school life to me was a happy, positive experience, I realize now that it may have been a very different experience for the Latino children of the community. In her book, *The Mexican Outsiders: A Community History of Marginalization and Discrimination*, one time Santa Paula resident Martha Menchaca writes about the institutional and de facto racism that characterized Santa Paula from the end of the nineteenth century well into the last years of the twentieth century. Menchaca came to Santa Paula from Mexico at age five with her parents

Me in 1962 at my 8th grade graduation from Isbell School. This is really a photo of a young girl between two worlds —13 years old and neither a child nor a woman.

in 1961, and went to Santa Paula schools until she was seventeen, going on to earn a PhD at Stanford.

For instance, I had gone to Barbara Webster School from 1957-1959. I had no idea that when it was built in 1925, it was originally named Canyon School. Constructed on the east side of Santa Paula in "Mexican Town," it was totally segregated. With eight classrooms, two restrooms and an office, the school served about 950 children. By comparison, Isbell School, built the same year on the northwest side of town for about the same number of Anglo children, had twenty-two classrooms, a cafeteria, an auditorium and several offices.

At the time, segregation was the law of the land, but even as that odious practice was excised, Santa Paula schools and residential neighborhoods con-tinued the practice of racial separation as much out of habit as official policy.

I will talk later about the role racial discrimination played in the early years of Limoneira's founding.

As a privileged white child I was unaware of these undercurrents. In elementary school, classes were not segregated, but as we progressed from being in a single classroom all day to taking subject matter from different teachers, class makeup was determined by test scores. This often resulted in a de facto form of segregation as kids for whom English was a second language were less likely to score well.

To me it was a golden time and I wished I could hold onto it forever—life at the ranch and summers on Faria Beach where it seemed everyone from Fillmore and Santa Paula went to escape the heat. The annual Fourth of July baseball game was played by a virtual who's who of west county families—Teague, Pidduck, Pinkerton, Samways, Wilde, Romney, Wileman, Munger and Stewart, on a beach so wide the ocean seemed a mile away.

There was also a European trip with mom and dad that took me out of school for six blissful weeks in 1961 at the end of my seventh-grade year. We visited Amsterdam, Paris, London, Edinburgh and Dublin on travel that was a business trip for dad and an incredible adventure and indelible learning experience for me.

On that trip we visited our Gamble relatives in Balleymoney, County Antrim in Northern Ireland. The Gamble sisters, Elizabeth and Rachel, came to Santa Paula to work for their uncle, John Pinkerton, in the late 1880s. Elizabeth (Lizzie) was my great-grandmother Munger.

If I can lay claim to having a broad perspective of history, to feel it as something personal and yet universally important, it was this trip that shaped me.

LEFT: The family gathered to celebrate Aunt Sarah's 90th birthday in 1958. The appearance is of a dignified and unified group, but that veneer would be torn away with Sarah's death five years later as the various family groups fought over disposition of her estate.

From L to R: Nathan Weston Blanchard III, Josephine Esther Blanchard (Grandma Tiny), Elizabeth Blanchard, Betsy (seated on the floor), Aunt Sarah, Elizabeth Kelsey Howie, Mary Howie (at her feet), Eliot Blanchard, (Four standing at back right, L to R) Kelly Howie, John Merriman, Amy Blanchard, John Blanchard.

Looking back, I realize this time signaled the end of an idyllic life that was soon to change. I can close my eyes and, through the glow of nostalgia, give you a guided tour of all thirty-plus rooms in *El Naranjal*, and with equal accuracy guide you through the five-stall Queen Anne marvel that was the coach barn, or the ten-stall mule barn and on and on through that world that with the death of Aunt Sarah in 1963, would soon cease to exist.

I can also remember with great fondness all of the people who worked for our family and who played such an important part of my childhood. They included: ranch foreman Justo Ayala and his beautiful wife, Carmen; the ranch crew Jess and Modesto; Aunt Sarah's chauffeur and *major domo*, Theo McAbee and his ailing wife Opal; Aune Lindholm, Aunt Sarah's Finnish cook

1961 dinner cruise on the Seine with my parents—what an experience for an almost 13-year-old. This trip, which included Holland, France and most of Great Britain, took me out of 7th grade for almost six weeks. The effect was incalculable in that it shaped my view of history and the world for the rest of my life.

and housekeeper; and our own cook-housekeeper-and-substitute mom, Kerttu Veholainen, also from Finland. Yes, they were employees, but a word from any one of them was to be regarded with the same authority as that of our parents.

The room where it happened…a photo of the room across the page where the family gathered in 1958 to celebrate Sarah's 90th Birthday.

I so remember family dinners here. The children's table was always beneath one of the south-facing window seats.

A view of the living room looking east. On the table is a gorgeous lamp made from a Chinese vase that now graces my living room as does the water clock on the wall next to the glass doors on the right. Note the gorgeous beamed ceilings.

Looking across the atrium from the dining room into the living room. On the walls are artifacts brought back from family travels plus some of the collection of Chumash baskets.

All photographs this page and next taken in 1963.

Another view across the atrium showing more of the many objects collected over the years.

View from the elegant dining room across the entry atrium.

Looking into the living room with another view of the glorious ceilings.

This part of the living room was really the heart of Aunt Sarah's home. I remember her there reading or holding court at Christmas time as the butler passed pre-dinner aperitifs—old fashioneds for the adults and apple juice for the children.

The "Other" Grandparents

I WISH YOU COULD HAVE KNOWN my wonderful paternal grandmother, Grandma Tiny, or maternal grandparents John and Ella Munger, or all the other aunts, uncles and cousins.

Most people think it is my Blanchard relations who have the long history in Ventura County, but my mother's Munger and Wileman families have equally deep roots.

Dexter Samuel Munger, my great-great grandfather, was born in Genesee County, New York in 1836. He enlisted in the Union Army in 1861, joining the 9th Michigan Cavalry. A portion of this regiment captured Jefferson Davis, the president of the Confederacy. The story goes that Davis was trying to escape Richmond, Virginia, disguised as a woman. Captain Munger thought the lady's feet looked awfully big, and delicately lifting her skirts with the tip of his sword, discovered the ruse. Or at least that's the story told in my family. I have since learned many other families claim that same story.

Dexter Munger was married in Orleans County, New York to Jennie Warren; they had two sons, Seymour and Burton Lorenzo. He came to California in 1876 with the two boys after the death of his wife. He died in Santa Paula in 1890 and is buried in the Santa Paula Cemetery.

Dexter's son, Burton Lorenzo, born in Mungerville, Michigan in 1858, came to Santa Paula with his father

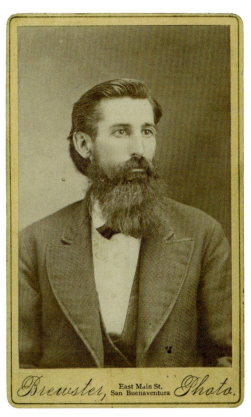

Captain Dexter Samuel Munger, my great-great-grandfather, was credited with capturing Confederate president Jefferson Davis as he fled Richmond disguised as a woman. Captain Munger thought the lady's feet appeared too big, and lifting her skirt with the tip of his sword, discovered the ruse.

Dexter Samuel's son, Burton Lorenzo Munger was born in Michigan, but came to California with his father and brother, Seymour, in 1876.

when he was seventeen. He worked for the Hardison-Stewart Oil Company, predecessor of Union Oil, and then managed the Hardison Horse and Cattle Company. He married Elizabeth Gamble and had three sons, Burton Lorenzo, Jr., Heathcot and my grandfather, John Pinkerton Munger. Their mother was Elizabeth Gamble of Balleymoney, County Antrim, Northern Ireland.

My grandfather, John Pinkerton Munger, continued the Munger tradition of fine-looking men. Grampa John and Grandma Ella, whom he married in 1914, were loving mainstays to my brothers and me.

Lizzie Gamble and her sister, Rachel, came to Ventura County in 1885 to cook for their uncle, John Pinkerton, who ran a gang of men drilling for oil on Sulphur Mountain in the Upper Ojai, between Ojai and Santa Paula.

I vaguely remember meeting Great-Granny Munger when I was a little child and she a very old lady. She lived with her son, my great uncle Heathcot, on the Munger Ranch just west of Santa Paula. She was very tall, over six feet, and apparently had feet to match, which greatly embarrassed her. As a result she always wore shoes that were too small and subsequently suffered terrible foot problems that she blamed on having had her feet stepped on by a horse.

The Mungers were all tall, a trait shared by my mother and her brother, Dr. John Roger, Ventura County's first dermatologist, and seen to this day in my tall, willowy daughter Devon. I remember one day when she was about nine, looking at a picture of her great-grandfather and his two brothers in bathing costumes on the Rincon. She wailed, "There are my legs!" not realizing then how lucky she was to have inherited those genes.

My daughter, Devon, at age 11, displaying those long, beautiful Munger legs! *Photo by John Blanchard.*

My great-grandfather, Thomas Wileman, a butcher by trade, came to California from Havre de Grace Maryland, after a chance visit by Ventura County Supervisor Rufus Touchston.

Thomas' wife, Isamiah, my Granny Wileman lived to be 104. She had two sisters, Hezekiah and Philippina. None of those biblical names has been carried forward by their Munger and Blanchard relatives.

In 1914, John Munger married Ella Wileman who had moved with her family to Santa Paula from Havre de Grace, Maryland. Grandma Ella was the sixth of seven children and the only girl. Her father, Thomas, was a butcher who decided to bring his family west after Rufus Touchston, a member of the Ventura County Board of Supervisors, happened to come into his shop and sang the praises of the county. Touchston left a calling card with his Santa Paula address, saying if they came west the family was welcome to stay with him. Little did Mr. Touchston know that Thomas, his wife, Isamiah Felty Wileman, and seven children would take him up on his offer. Thomas bundled up his family and took a train across the country to Santa Paula, having no other connection to the area. He set up a butcher business and bartered his services to feed and clothe his family. The family's connection with Rufus Touchston was to endure for many years.

Thomas died in 1916, when the team of horses he was driving was frightened by a train whistle. They ran away and plunged into a barranca, killing him. I remember his widow, Granny Wileman, who died in 1961, at the age of 104.

My brothers and I adored Grampa John and Grandma Ella Munger. Most Sundays our family went to their house for chicken dinner, with the best mashed potatoes and gravy. The house was cozy and welcoming, quite unlike the grander homes of our Blanchard relatives.

Grandma Ella let me play in her flour bin. How I loved the silky feel of the flour as it ran through my fingers. She also had a huge collection of *Better Homes and Gardens* magazines. I would settle in on the couch, chocolate chip cookie in hand, and spend hours poring over them.

Grampa John was a fine looking man with wonderful blue eyes. He ran the Signal Gas Station in Santa Paula and then went to work for the County of Ventura, first in Weights and Measures and then in Flood Control. My brother John remembers going with Grampa John as he conducted spot inspections of the weights at county gas stations, affixing a bright yellow sticker on compliant pumps. I loved hearing about his fleet of 'dozers as they were called out to widen flood control channels and other such work. He was always interested

Four generations from L to R: Great Granny Wileman, Grandma Ella and my mother, Elizabeth, holding me in 1948.

Grandpa John Pinkerton Munger was the most loving grandparent one could have wished for, yet he let me know if I did something that disappointed him.

in the sports I was involved with, whether riding or swimming. He didn't expect me to win all the time, but he did expect me to do my best.

I remember pulling out of a swimming race once, feigning a foot cramp, but really because I wasn't in shape and just got tired. He didn't need to say anything, the look of disappointment he gave me was enough.

If the Blanchard relatives were the ones with "position" in the community, my Munger relatives, especially my grandparents, were the ones most grounded in the reality of living in that community. To them, your value was not based on some unearned family connection, but rather on the results of your own commitment to decency and honest work.

On the Blanchard side of the family, it was Josephine Esther Blanchard, Grandma Tiny, Nathan, Jr.'s second wife, who was our favorite.

Her own family story was remarkable as her parents, James Long McClelland and Sophia Byrd McClelland, were both medical doctors. Sophia's father, Jesse Byrd of Virginia, was a staunch south-

My paternal great-grandparents, Sophia Byrd and James Long McClelland, were both medical doctors, graduating in 1884 from Cooper Medical School (precursor of Stanford Medical School) and going to Chicago for further training at Physicians and Surgeons Medical College.

I love this seemingly candid portrait of the McClelland family. Grandmother Sophia pets Shep, James stretches out his long legs, Esther, (Grandma Tiny) looks dreamily into the camera while Isabelle seems to be admiring herself in a mirror, (unless she's checking her cellphone messages?).

erner and opposed his daughter's marriage to a Yankee from Pennsylvania, so the young couple eloped in July 1878. Sophia lost her first child at birth from want of a doctor in attendance, a circumstance that certainly contributed to her and her husband both attending Cooper Medical School (now Stanford Medical School) in 1884 and another two years of training at the Chicago Physicians and Surgeons Medical College.[7]

Returning west to practice, they moved around the Central Valley, finally settling in Los Banos.

Grandma Tiny was born in Oakland, just before her parents moved to Chicago for medical training. She attributed her short stature—she was 4'10"—to lack of good nutrition during her parents' early peripatetic years.

Esther, as she was called, spent two years at the San Jose State Normal School, graduating with a teaching certificate in 1905. The president of the school found a possible job opening in Santa Paula. Grandma Tiny was interviewed for the position by none other than her future father-in-law, Nathan Weston Blanchard. She got the job and married Nathan Weston Blanchard, Jr. on February 8, 1908.

I know that date so well. It is engraved inside her wedding band that I wear, alongside my own, as I write this.

[7] Dean Blanchard, *Of California's First Citrus Empire*, 37-38.

Grandma Tiny wrote poetry, played the piano, guitar and violin, and sang. I remember her coming to visit us at the home that had once been hers. She would open the front door and sing out "Who, whooo?" and any child or dog or cat within earshot would come running to her.[8]

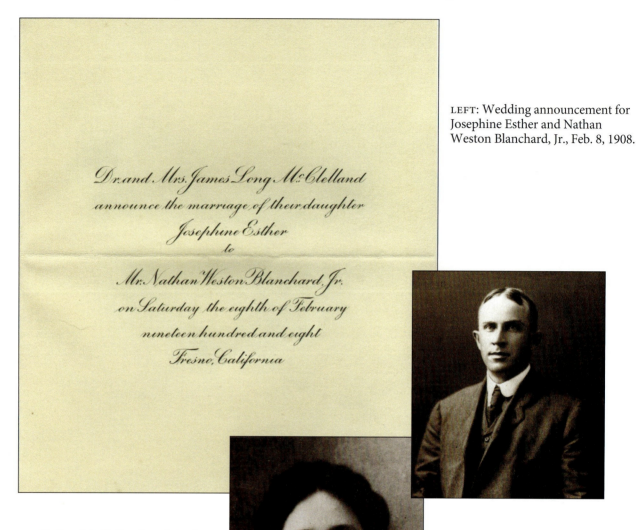

LEFT: Wedding announcement for Josephine Esther and Nathan Weston Blanchard, Jr., Feb. 8, 1908.

Dr. and Mrs. James Long McClelland
announce the marriage of their daughter
Josephine Esther
to
Mr. Nathan Weston Blanchard, Jr.
on Saturday the eighth of February
nineteen hundred and eight
Fresno, California

RIGHT: Esther McClelland and Nathan Weston Blanchard, Jr. about the time of their wedding. Esther had arrived in 1905 to teach school in Santa Paula. She was interviewed for her job by her future father-in-law. When she and NWB, Jr. were married, she was 22 and he was 32.

---

[8] My mother loved her dearly, and said this in a speech to the Santa Paula Historical Society in 1988: "My mother-in-law, Grandma Tiny, loved me like a daughter and I was happy to return that love. There was nothing she would not do for her children or grandchildren or her church. I will always remember her for her warmth, her musical ability and her great charm….The Blanchard men left their marks about the community, but these two women (also including Aunt Sarah) left their marks on the Blanchard descendants."

The Black Sheep or Lost Sheep?

THE ONE PERSON you don't hear much about, even in the book by his own son, Dean Hobbs Blanchard, was my grandfather, Nathan Weston Blanchard, Jr., who was born October 16, 1873 in Santa Paula.

As a privileged son of the area, he became a member of the Jonathan Club of Los Angeles, vice-president of the Limoneira Company, president of the N.W. Blanchard Investment Company and member of the executive board of the first branch of the Pacific-Southwest Trust & Savings Bank of Santa Paula.

He died in 1932 at the age of fifty-eight, on the 10th hole of the Ojai Valley Inn golf course, after eating a substantial lunch. His obituary read, "His many friends and neighbors in this community who have shared his acquaintance these many years, and have known his inner life, whether in the home, the lodge, the many benevolent associations, or in the field of sports, will miss his kind, genial and generous personality."

So far so good, but I think it is his "inner life" that is so much more interesting. There is the story of his running away from the Thacher School in 1891.

This is a copy of the infamous expulsion letter from Thacher School headmaster, Sherman Day Thacher. He hopes that the communication would neither offend Nathan, Jr.'s parents nor cause a rift in their personal relationship. Hard to see how the relationship would not be affected since Thacher called their son a liar and a cheat!

He made his way down Santa Paula Creek back to town where his mother, Ann Elizabeth, hid him in the attic of *El Naranjal* for three days in fear of Nathan Sr.'s temper when he found out.

There is a remarkable letter to great-grandfather from Thacher's founder, Sherman Day Thacher, in which the headmaster basically says…if I never see your kid again it's too soon…but I hope we can always be friends.

The letter must have worked. My father and his two brothers all went to Thacher, as did a grandson, Robin, my own daughter Devon, a great-granddaughter, and great-great grandsons, Jack and Sam Richardson.

Then there was the elopement…but, when was this and to whom? The story I heard growing up was that the woman was of little regard and great grandfather was livid. He supposedly went after the renegade, brought him home and had the marriage annulled.

I have since had the opportunity to read letters and family diaries from the time that are archived in the Research Library of the Museum of Ventura County. There was much, much more going on than I ever knew. The following information was gleaned from those letters and diaries in the museum collection.

For instance, I learned that after Thacher, grandfather was sent to the Belmont School near San Francisco in June of 1891. The headmaster, Mr. T.J. Reid, declared that his methods were very different from Mr. Thacher's, who for instance, had let young Nathan, Jr. go into the "village" of Ojai each afternoon. That kind of freedom came to end.

Grandfather's letters home to his mother and sister, Sarah, were those of a miserable and very homesick young man. In a letter to Sarah, he mentions that his roommate had just been expelled. One wonders what kind of school this was; some kind of nineteenth century boot camp? In fact, although not technically a military academy, the school required three hours of military drills each week.[9]

In a letter to his wife, Nathan Sr., obviously frustrated, speaks disparagingly of his son. "Nathan is not a considerate boy, and not self-reliant." He laments that his nephew, son of brother-in–law Judge Charles Fernald, was going to Stanford, something to which Nathan, Jr. could not aspire. While Nathan was still at Thacher, his father offered him $1 for each book he read, but then added he had to do the reading under supervision as NWB didn't trust the boy to do it properly.

In another letter NWB tells his wife that Nathan continues to smoke, "...even 'though I offered him $500 to not smoke until he was 21." Bribery didn't seem to work with young Nathan.

_____

[9] Porter E. Sargent, *A Handbook of American Private Schools* (1916), 144-145.

How I wish I could have known great-grandmother Ann Elizabeth. All her pictures show her as a pleasant, smiling lady, unusual at the time of stern and unsmiling portraits. There is a story of her going from Santa Paula to Ventura to see the dentist because of her bad teeth. She had eleven teeth removed sans anesthetic. The lady who took care of the children while she was away said, "Mrs. Blanchard left a young woman, and returned an old one."

In a remarkable letter from the Belmont School Headmaster, Professor Reid, to Nathan's mother, Ann Elizabeth, dated September 1891, Reid gives the OK for her to visit with her son. He says,

> It is altogether best that he should spend Sunday with you. If he were going with a weak and yielding mother I should advise just the other way, but when the mother, after the manner of the Spartan mother says, 'Come home with your shield or on it,' it is good for a son to get into such an atmosphere.

Nathan, however, returned to Santa Paula after a very short stay at Belmont. This was the end of his formal education.

As for the elopement, Nathan, Jr. and Mary Grace Fernald (no known relation to the Santa Barbara Fernalds) were married in Alameda County, California, June of 1897. The marriage was not annulled—in fact, they remained together until 1905.

Far from being a woman of inappropriate background, Grace came from a family of good standing in Santa Paula. Her father, Captain Charles Fernald, held several important positions in town, including that of postmaster in 1907, and was also a member of the elite Santa Paula Rifle Club, of which C.C. Teague was also a member.

In July, just a month after the elopement, Ann Elizabeth in a letter to her daughter, Eunice, urges acceptance. "Dear Eunice, I am glad that we have done right by Grace. This is a motherless girl, a poor girl...." In the same letter, Ann Elizabeth goes on to say that she has discovered Grace had kidney problems that have been going on for two years. "Poor child—if she had had a mother that would not have been going on all this time without attention. Her mother died of Bright's Disease of the kidneys and it seems that she has a haunting feeling that she will have the same trouble."[10]

There seems to be a lot going on in this letter that perhaps leads up to great-grandmother's urging acceptance of the elopement. A few sentences earlier she laments. "I have sat in sack cloth and ashes and felt oh if I had done everything that was right and that in some way it must be the fault of my bringing up that Nathan is as he is. God has taken away from me two beautiful sons—But I bow my head in thankfulness that they are_safe_—I might have made such a failure with them—God only knows."[11]

Poor lady, she seems to feel responsible for her son's behavior. Does she feel on the one hand she has spoiled her son, or on the other, been too hard on him? Is she urging acceptance of the elopement as some kind of atonement for her treatment of Nathan?

The family, although they considered Grace very sweet and applauded her "simple manners," according to a letter from great-grandmother to Grace, they definitely didn't think she was up to the job of being a Blanchard. Ann Elizabeth told Grace the family wanted her to go away to a girl's school either in Berkeley or in San Francisco for a year to prepare her for the "path that lay ahead."

Grace never went away to school, and they were divorced in 1905. I had hoped the diaries of my Aunt Sarah would provide some enlightenment, but Sarah was a very laconic diarist. She was not introspective, speculative or gossipy. The only mention of the couple was to state several times, "Nathan and Grace came to dinner." By the middle of 1904, Grace ceases to be mentioned.

Grace left Santa Paula for San Francisco at some point after the divorce. She kept the Blanchard name. She became a court stenographer and then a resident nurse at the Mt. Zion Hospital. She died, age sixty-eight, in 1944, and is buried in the Santa Paula Cemetery, although not in the Blanchard plot.

I cannot remember my father mentioning his father. My mother said she only met Nathan, Jr. once before he died, and she described him as a detached and distant man. According to my mother, Eliot and his two brothers did not know about this first marriage until they were young adults, after the death of their father in 1932.

I have not found much else, but I have heard Nathan, Jr. was well known for the high stakes poker games he presided over upstairs in the Glen Tavern, in Santa Paula, which was built in 1911.

---

[10] This is very interesting and perhaps explains why Nathan and Grace were childless throughout their eight-year marriage. Bright's Disease is known to cause infertility.

[11] She lost her first-born, Dean Hobbs Blanchard, in 1871, and her last-born, Thomas Goodwin Blanchard, in 1876.

I like to think Nathan, Jr. was a bit like Queen Victoria's playboy son, "Bertie," who became Edward VII after her death in 1901. Both were the sons of formidable, straight-laced parents who, frankly, were tough acts to follow. Perhaps Nathan Weston Blanchard, Jr. and Edward VII were kindred souls, striking out at pre-ordained lives in the only ways they could?

The Blanchards traveled widely including to Europe, especially Vienna, to Russia and Persia (now Iran) as well as to the South Seas. Here they prepare to board the *SS Manolo* in 1930. I am fortunate to have wonderful old Persian rugs brought back from a trip in 1906. L to R: NWB, Jr., Grandma Tiny, Dad, Dean and Weston.

I can't but comment that my father and his brothers were wonderfully handsome! L to R: Eliot, Dean and Weston in 1931, the year before their father died.

End of an Era

MY BROTHERS AND I loved our life in Santa Paula, but it was, in fact, a little semi-feudal world shaped by the lemon and orange orchards that created it and would very soon be overtaken by events taking place within the family and in the outside world.

In 1963, after one year at Santa Paula High School, I was sent to the very proper Bishop's School, a girl's boarding school in La Jolla.

I lived through the early years of the '60s at a school that was still Victorian in nature. We wore hats and gloves to travel, even on the Greyhound bus. Coffee was allowed only as a senior privilege, and we went everywhere in La Jolla in carefully chaperoned groups, like a flock of obedient little ducks.

Although I received a very fine and sophisticated education, it was the end of being bold and fearless; the end of my free-wheeling-animal-filled life on the ranch. It was as if I stepped out of the world I knew and into a very different one. The problem was that when I tried return to my life, it was gone; it had quite literally vanished.

That same year, 1963, Aunt Sarah died and the extended family I thought was so tight and loving disintegrated. Sarah had left a will that scrupulously allocated her financial wealth, but was silent as how to distribute the riches that had surrounded her in *El Naranjal*.

Aunt Sarah in 1948 on the occasion of her 80th birthday.

Sarah signing copies of her book *Memories of a Child's Early California Days*, in 1961.

El Naranjal was first constructed in about 1876 as the home of the Blanchard Ranch foreman. Over the years it was transformed into the family's home that was gracious, elegant and yet welcoming. In 1966, five years after this photo was taken, the magnificent home was razed to the ground.

Valuable artwork, furniture, Persian rugs, silver and crystal became sources of friction and worse. The beautiful museum-quality Royal Cantonese dinner settings and serving pieces that had been brought to the family as gifts by succeeding generations of Chinese employees became battlegrounds.

The family never really recovered and then two years later, in 1965, my father, Eliot, and beloved grandfather, John Munger, died within a month of each other. I was seventeen and devastated, but I am ashamed to say I was largely oblivious to the anguish of the person most affected, my mother. I am forever grateful to her for the way she carried on for us, loved and guided us, and shepherded the legacy that was left for her to manage in the trust that would come to us at her death in 2009.

Aunt Sarah's death left the family with decisions regarding her home and the rest of her property. We offered *El Naranjal* to the city of Santa Paula, but the city declined, saying they had their hands full managing the Union Oil Museum in town. There was a plan to move the coach barn up to Steckle Park, but a suspicious fire burned it to the ground.

A group of local investors bought the property intending to build a dozen or so large estate homes. To this day I weep when I remember how *El Naranjal* was razed to the ground. A recession soon followed the purchase of the property and the estate homes were never built. The lovely gardens and beautiful old trees, unwatered and untended, were left to decay.

Looking back, I realize this was an era, at least in our little corner of the world, where the concept of historical preservation had not yet dawned, but to me, it was as if my world had come crashing around me.

My Parents

I DON'T KNOW HOW my parents met. Dad was born July 7, 1914 in Santa Paula and mother, March 18, 1917, about nine miles away in Bardsdale, a tiny burg nestled alongside the Santa Clara River adjacent to Fillmore. Mom and her parents, John and Ella Munger, and older brother, Roger, lived in Bardsdale until she was eleven.

In 1928, they moved into Santa Paula just before the collapse of the St. Francis Dam, a catastrophe that killed over 400 people. Mother said they were awakened in the middle of the night by lights flashing below them near the Santa Clara River. Her father, Grampa John, got in the car and drove down to investigate. When he returned he told the family, "Some dam broke somewhere," and they all went back to bed. Few people even knew of the existence of the big dam up San Francisquito Canyon until it broke causing one of the worst man-made disasters in California history, second in deaths only to the 1906 San Francisco earthquake and fire.

Santa Paula was a small town and my parents must have known each other from grade school days. I know mom went up to dances at Thacher School where dad was a student. She attended Santa Paula High School, graduating in 1933. She attended Holmby College in Los Angeles, graduating in 1935, and then returned to Santa Paula where she worked two years at the Security Pacific Bank.

Elizabeth Munger was named Santa Paula High School's May Queen in 1933. Her flower-bedecked wicker throne in fact came from the veranda of the Blanchard home.

Eliot Blanchard, captain of the Thacher baseball team in 1931.

(*continued on page 47*)

Elizabeth Munger, second from right bottom row, in her junior year at Santa Paula High School. She was class vice president and editor of both the year book, *El Solano* and the student newspaper, *The Cardinal.*

Commencement Exercises

Holmby College

Los Angeles

June Eleventh
Nineteen Hundred and Thirty-Four
at Three O'clock

Holmby College commencement program and Elizabeth's Cap and Gown certificate, 1934. She graduated the following year, in 1935.

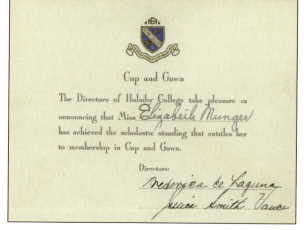

Cap and Gown

The Directors of Holmby College take pleasure in announcing that Miss *Elizabeth Munger* has achieved the scholastic standing that entitles her to membership in Cap and Gown.

Directors:

Frederica de Laguna

Julia Smith Vance

Wow! Mom at Faria beach in 1935. Photo by Vernon Freeman.

It's often difficult to look at our parents and imagine them young and in love. This photo in 1933 should dispel such notions!

Mr. and Mrs. John Pinkerton Munger

announce the marriage of their daughter

Elizabeth Irene
to
Mr. Eliot McClelland Blanchard

on Saturday, the nineteenth of June

One thousand, nine hundred and thirty-seven

Santa Paula, California

At Home
Palo Alto, California

Mom and dad's wedding announcement.

Formal wedding portrait of mom with her parents John and Ella Munger at the Bardsdale Methodist Church in 1937.

The wedding party L to R: Weston Blanchard, Ruthie Dunn, John Roger Munger, the bride and groom, Madge McFarland and Dean Blanchard.

BELOW: Brochure from the Roma, the ship on which they sailed on their magical first class honeymoon voyage of the Mediterranean.

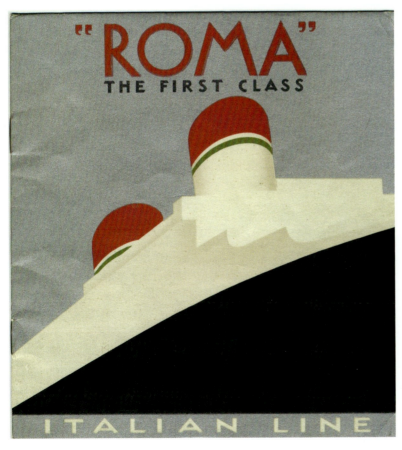

Dad was already at Stanford, but he must have returned home often to woo the beautiful Elizabeth Munger.

They were married at the Bardsdale Methodist Church in June 1937, and following what must have been an amazing honeymoon to New York and then on to the Mediterranean aboard the *SS Roma*, they both went to Stanford. Eliot graduated from Stanford Law School in 1939 and Elizabeth got her bachelor of arts degree that same year, graduating with triple majors in history, journalism, and economics.

They lived in Beverly Hills the first years of their marriage, where dad practiced law until the United States went to war in 1941.

My Parents **47**

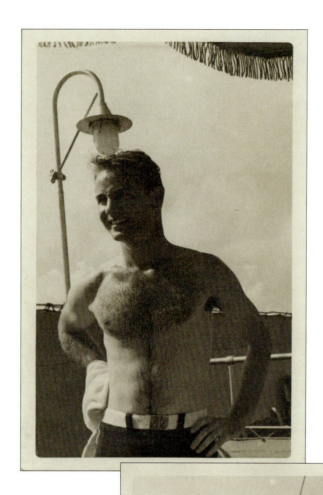

My parents enjoy the pleasures of First Class aboard the Italian ship Roma on their honeymoon in 1937. Looking like something out of Hollywood Central Casting, they were so young, so beautiful and so unaware that they were experiencing the twilight of privileged life before World War II.

PASSPORT

UNITED STATES OF AMERICA

Photograph of bearer

Eliot McClelland Blanchard

PHOTOGRAPH ATTACHED

DEPARTMENT OF STATE

This passport, properly visaed, is valid for travel in all countries unless otherwise specified.

This passport, unless limited to a shorter period, is valid for two years from its date of issue and may be renewed for an additional period of two years.

Limitations

This passport is not valid for travel in SPAIN

Este pasaporte no es válido para viajar en ESPAÑA

Ce passeport n'est pas valable pour voyages en ESPAGNE

4

5

My parents traveled under a single passport dated June 21, 1937. It reads "Eliot McClelland Blanchard a citizen of the United States. The bearer is accompanied by his wife, Elizabeth." The passport is stamped at the various exotic ports of call the Roma visited—France, Italy, Egypt, by the British Passport Control Office on their visa to enter in Palestine, Beyrouth, (under French jurisdiction) and Istanbul. Thirty-one years later, as a recent widow, my mother retraced her honeymoon voyage when she came to visit me in the summer 1968 while I was in Israel. While on that Mediterranean cruise she met a charming Englishman named Charles Neal. They were married in 1971.

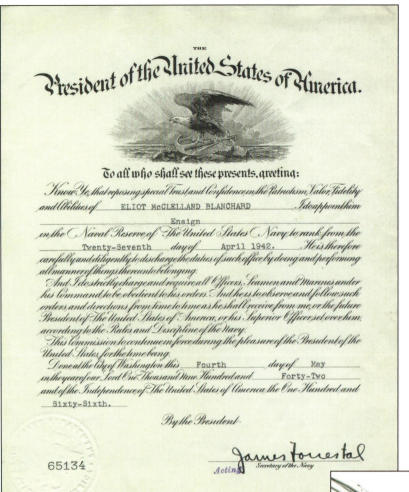

ABOVE: Dad's enlistment papers in the U.S. Naval Reserve as an Ensign in 1942.

papers, saying, after all, he had been signing every other document for the commander.

He served in the Pacific, including some time at the end of the war in Guam.

Returning from the war, Eliot fully intended to continue his Beverly Hills law practice. Both of my brothers had been born and life seemed pointed in that direction as he and Elizabeth enjoyed life in Beverly Hills. He then got a job offer that would quite upend their plans.

He was hired in 1946 by The Samuel Edwards Associates in Santa Paula as general manager in charge of their agriculture and oil properties, a job he would hold until his death in 1965.

He enlisted in the Navy Reserve as an Ensign and was stationed at the Port of Long Beach—not where he wanted to be. His commanding officer had a ranch in Escondido where he spent most of his time, leaving the day-to-day running of the Port to dad.

The commanding officer refused to sign dad's transfer papers, not wanting to ruffle his comfortable life. Eliot finally signed his own transfer

RIGHT: Ensign Blanchard displaying his usual casual grace aboard ship.

ABOVE: Dad spent some time in Guam at the end of the war in the Pacific. It was a precarious time as there were snipers holed up in the jungle who did not know or would not acknowledge the war had ended.

Typical of life in the 1950s and '60s, my father concentrated on work while mom managed the home front. She was outgoing, a joiner and an organizer, while dad was much more reserved and emotionally distant. That began to change in 1963 with the birth of my brother John and wife Pam's first daughter, Jennifer.

RIGHT: Dad's Navy discharge papers, February 1946.

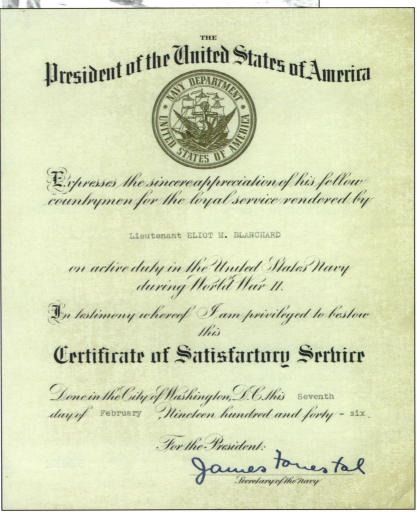

THE

President of the United States of America

Expresses the sincere appreciation of his fellow countrymen for the loyal service rendered by

Lieutenant ELIOT M. BLANCHARD

on active duty in the United States Navy during World War II.

In testimony whereof I am privileged to bestow this

Certificate of Satisfactory Service

Done in the City of Washington, D.C. this Seventh day of February, Nineteen hundred and forty - six.

For the President:

James Forrestal
Secretary of the Navy

Dad's pictures are usually very sober, but this one, taken at a Hawaiian luau in 1963, shows his happy, devilish side. He loved the Hawaiian Islands and I think he and mom would have bought a vacation home there had not his untimely death in 1965 shattered those dreams.

Dad seemed to experience an emotional thaw. He became much more relaxed and approachable. In April 1965, he came down to visit me at Bishop's, unusual as he usually came with mom. He stayed at the beautiful La Valencia Hotel in La Jolla. I have this lovely memory of him sitting in a chair in the garden of the hotel before he took me and three friends out to dinner. He sat in that chair beaming as we four twined around him like dryads 'round an oak.

He probably never before had quite that kind of attention. The moment passed, never to be duplicated, as he died of a heart attack less than three months later, just a week after his 51st birthday.

Picture smiling faintly in a frame

Now only memories remain

Of the man you once were

Of the man you still are to me

Days turn to weeks, weeks into years

All still punctuated by tears

Picture smiling faintly in a frame

Now only memories remain...

Poem I wrote for my father my senior year in high school in 1965, just a few months after he died.

Off to see the world! Five of us Santa Paula girls at LAX heading to different destinations around the word. L to R: Chris Fox, Donna Crouch, me, Linda Stine and Vicki Tubbs.

Dad had an earlier heart attack in June 1965. He was recuperating in the hospital the last time I saw him. I left just a few days later to go to Norway as an exchange student with The Experiment in International Living, a program that sent young people around the world to experience family life abroad. I look back now and wonder how I could have left with my father in the hospital so ill, but realize that as a teenager I had little control over my life, and certainly not the power to change decisions that had already been made.

Mother took me to the airport and, as parents could in those days, walked out on the tarmac with me to the passenger stairs up into the plane. As I started up the stairs she said to me, "Betsy, your grandfather died last night."

What a send-off. Looking back, I can't believe she handled telling me about the death of her beloved father, my dear Grampa John, in this way. But the story only got stranger.

I stayed in Norway with the Bøe family in a little town called Tonsberg, about sixty miles south of Oslo on the western side of the Oslo Fjord.

I had returned to the Bøe farm after a two-week trip around Norway with my Norwegian sister, Marit, and the other Americans and their Norwegian sisters and brothers in my group. A big pile of letters awaited me. One was addressed to my Norwegian parents in my mother's distinctive hand. They, speaking no English, had not opened it so I did. The first line asked the Norwegians to tell me that my dear father had died. As I read this out, they all fell apart and I had to calm them.

Dad had been gone for two weeks before I knew about it. All I wanted to do was get on a phone and talk to my mother. The Bøe household wasn't equipped to handle an international call, so Mrs. Bøe, who really didn't drive, drove me into town to the home of my American group leader.

A harrowing trip ensued, during which Mrs. Bøe passed a truck—right into the path of an oncoming car. Both the truck and the other car swerved off into ditches on either side of the road, while Mrs. Bøe, never flinching, barreled down the middle of the road towards town.

I made the call and talked to my mother. At seventeen, all I really wanted was to be told what to do. Mom thought for a moment and then said, "I think your father would have wanted you to stay."

For me, that was as good as an order. I stayed for four miserable weeks where I was mentally neither part of the group in Norway, nor home able to grieve with my family. When I reached home, dad had been gone for six weeks and everyone else had moved on to another phase of mourning. I felt completely alone and emotionally numb.

Myself and Mrs. Gertrude Keeler on graduation day. She introduced me to modern European history, a subject I loved and in which I received a Masters Degree from USC in 1972.

My senior year in high school was to start shortly. I would have preferred to stay home and finish at Santa Paula High School, but my mother nixed that idea, saying it would jeopardize my chances of getting into a good college.

As a result, my senior year was an awful blur. I did poorly on my SAT's, so instead of going to some elite eastern school I went to USC, which in those days was not as hard to get into as it is today. I felt I had disappointed everyone. When the family gathered for my graduation from Bishop's I felt embarrassed that they had come to witness my failure.

As it turned out, USC was probably the best place for me. I wasn't particularly challenged academically, so I had a chance to make some dubious choices in boyfriends, party, drink and get bad grades the first semester. I pulled out of my downward spiral the second part of the year and had a pretty decent college career after that.

My graduation photo at Bishop's School, 1966.

Pi Beta Phi and Delta Tau Delta party freshman year at USC. I remember it was a great party, but don't remember the boys!

Looking back, I realize that my mother was very much influenced by her own background—the poor, but beautiful girl who married into the town "royalty" so to speak. She was always trying to live up to what she thought was expected of her and also of her family, thus her insistence I return to the Bishop's School rather than finish my senior year at Santa Paula High School.

In 1968, historian Michael Belknap wrote a short paper about the influence of the lemon industry, both good and bad, on Santa Paula. He talked about the town's reliance on the philanthropy of the growers, but also about the aura of prestige that surrounded them. To me this account encapsulates my mother's dilemma. Was she characterized by her own accomplishments or by the fact that she was married to a Blanchard?

The importance of rancher social prestige as a factor in Santa Paula politics was also demonstrated in school elections held in 1958 and 1959. In the former year the elementary schools secured passage of a tax override. Success was achieved, in the opinion of Dr. Robert Belknap, district superintendent at that time, primarily because Eliot Blanchard's wife, Elizabeth, campaigned for the measure. At about the same time, the high school district bond issue for site acquisition was twice defeated by the voters. Mrs. Blanchard became convinced that high school affairs were being poorly managed and decided to run for the board. In the election which followed, although all candidates adopted essentially the same position and none was tainted by previous connection with the board, Mrs. Blanchard polled almost two hundred more votes than her three opponents combined. The decisive factor in (both) election(s) appears to have been the Blanchard name.[12]

I don't know if Elizabeth thought deeply about this. I doubt it. Rather she likely accepted it as, "just the way things were."

I remember another telling incident in the summer of 1958, when some friends and I took an empty coffee can and went around the neighborhood collecting money, "for the crippled children." Mother was horrified of what people might think of her daughter out begging and hauled all three of us over to the Cerebral Palsy School in Santa Paula, where we turned over the few dollars we had collected.

We had no intention of keeping that money, although I don't think at nine or ten we had a clear idea of how to get it to "the crippled children." But rather than laud our intentions and make it into

---

[12] Michael Belknap, "The Era of the Lemon: A History of Santa Paula, California," *California Historical Society Quarterly* (June 1968): 131.

This photo captures the perfect definition of a "white gloves tea party." L-R: Theda Stewart; her mother, Mrs. Call; Elizabeth; Grandma Tiny and Grandma Ella, 1955.

Council and was later the president of the board of directors. She served 22 years on the Juvenile Justice Commission of Ventura County. Towards the end of her life she was honored by many organizations and by the City of Santa Paula. But my favorite memory of Elizabeth Munger Blanchard Neal, my mother, is finishing strong at age 80 at the Annual CROP Walk (*see page 58*) after a long and remarkable life.

"a teaching moment," all that concerned her was what people might think.

Given that rocky start, I think it is a miracle that I made a career in nonprofit fundraising!

Elizabeth remarried five years after Eliot's death to Charles Neal, a charming and charismatic Englishman. Charles moved to Santa Paula and the two had four wonderful years together before he, too, died leaving my mother twice-widowed in ten years.

Mom spent the next thirty years involved in the community, including work with Interface Children and Family Services and the Museum of Ventura County, where she both headed the Docent

In 1956, the Glen City Elementary School in Santa Paula was given an F84 B Thunder Jet for its playground by the U.S. Air Force. On hand to accept the gift were Ray Denlay, District Superintendent, Elizabeth Blanchard, Clerk of the School Board and Clifford Tanner, Glen City Student Body President.

Elizabeth Blanchard and Charles Neal, center, are married in 1971 at St. Giles Church, Leatherhead, England. They are flanked on the left by Charles' daughter, Angela, and on the right by best man, Jack Pearce.

Probably the best wedding reception picture ever! Mother and Charles exchange a rather passionate kiss, scandalizing or amusing the assembled guests!

Photos this page by H.C. Harridge.

My Parents 57

This photo of Elizabeth showing off skis and ski accessories ran in *Sunset Magazine* January, 1964.

Finishing strong! Elizabeth at 80 crossing the finish line of an annual CROP Walk. Although she was to live another twelve years, this picture best captures her true spirit and zest for life.

Great-grandfather Comes West

THE SANTA CLARA VALLEY is as pretty a piece of Southern California as one can imagine. And that's what my great-grandfather, Nathan Weston Blanchard, thought when he first traveled through in 1863. He, like many others who traveled west at that time, was particularly impressed by the year-round flowing Santa Clara River, surrounded by gentle hills rising to picturesque mountains and land that sustained growths of wild mustard that grew higher than his horse's head. Rich, fertile, well-watered land surrounded by natural beauty and blessed with a mild climate, would prove perfect to grow both crops and people.

Nathan Weston Blanchard was born in Madison, Maine in 1831, the son of Merrill Blanchard and Eunice Weston. His early life was spent working on his father's farm and when he was twelve, following the death of his mother, on the farm of his grandfather on the Kennebec River. At seventeen he prepared for college by working on the farm and teaching school. In 1851, at twenty, he entered Waterville College, now Colby College.

He managed his first two years of college teaching at three different schools, plus doing farm work. In 1854, he followed his father to California where he hoped to make enough money within two years

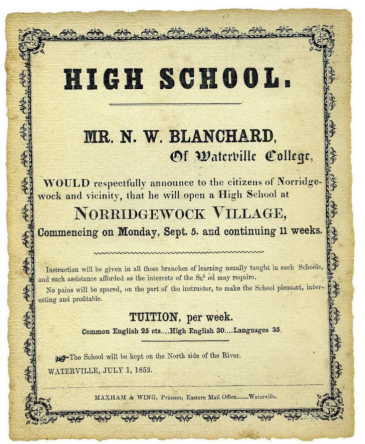

The handbill advertising NWB's high school in Waterville, Maine. It is dated July 1, 1853, a little more than a year before he sailed to California. He hoped to make enough money to return to Maine and finish his college education within two years. It would be ten years before he was able to return.

to continue his education. Alas, it would be ten years before he returned again to Maine.

A journey to California in 1854 was arduous at best, but young Nathan was tested early on when the steamer he booked encountered a huge storm and had to limp in to Norfolk, Virginia, her bulwarks caved in and coal fires extinguished. He waited there until another steamer from New York, the *Empire City*, took the now greatly reduced number of passengers on to Aspinwall, now Colon, in Panama.

From there he took the half-finished railway midway across the Isthmus and then continued on mule back to the Pacific. Nathan boarded the steam-

Nathan Weston Blanchard about 20 years old.

Great-great grandfather Merrill Blanchard.

ship, *Columbia*, nicknamed "The Rolling Moses," and landed in San Francisco on March 3, 1854.[13]

Young Nathan headed to the gold fields, to Tuolumne County, where his first mining venture at Tennessee Gulch was a dismal failure. His other attempts weren't any more successful. His journal recounts days of hard work and boredom, and the debts just kept piling up. The journal is an interesting account of not much—weather reports, scrupulous accounting of his finances, tales of a local shooting, and plans for self-improvement.

Great Grandpa wasn't a drinker, but it appears he liked to gamble a bit.[14]

Soon after his arrival in California, Nathan was joined by his father, Merrill, who had come west in 1851, and had been living in Oregon with his brother, Dean.[15] They evidently worked some mining claims together, but it is hard to understand their relationship. At one point Nathan wrote his

[13] *American Families: Genealogical and Biographical from Most Authentic Sources Including Much Valuable Material Drawn from Hitherto Unpublished Family Records with Accurate Reproduction and Description of Ancient Emblazonry Compiled by Master of Genealogic and Heraldic Science…*(c.1924).

[14] NWB's journal had been given to the Huntington Library in 1961 by my Aunt Sarah. I received a copy of it and thank my editor, Charles Johnson, for his efforts to make NWB's writing from 167 years ago legible.

[15] Lots of Deans in my narrative. There is Dean, the brother of NWB, Dean, NWB's son and another Dean, NWB's grandson.

Sadly, life in California was not for Merrill, and in a journal entry dated almost two years later, August 26, 1856, his son writes, "Father came here yesterday night last and left this afternoon intending to go home as soon as he can raise the money—He has been in this country almost five years & now with a down heart he goes home with the assistance of Dean [Merrill's brother] and myself." —a poignant requiem probably not unique at the time.

NWB's brother Dean Hobbs Blanchard. Dean seemed to be everyone's favorite uncle. Given this picture of a handsome and seemingly pleasant man, one can understand why.

A page from NWB's diary from his early days in the California gold fields. Dated August 26, 1856, it tells of his father Merrill's decision to leave California and return to Maine.
Courtesy The Huntington Library.

stepmother about, "Father's Anxiety, Misfortune and habits —," but gives no details.[16]

Later Nathan mentions "Father has gone to butchering with Jno. Kneeland a 'Down Easter' & is doing a good business,—I think." Nathan himself was to go to work for Kneeland in October 1854, and stayed with the meat market business as bookkeeper and clerk for several years, eventually becoming a partner in the business in 1859.

---

[16] The following journal entries are from the Journal of Nathan Weston Blanchard, The Huntington Library, mssHM 91475.

Merrill Blanchard's headstone, Lakeview Cemetery, Seattle, Washington.

The Illusive Merrill Blanchard

GREAT-GREAT GRANDFATHER Merrill has been hard, historically, to pin down. We hear of him returning to Maine in 1856, but then what? I was puzzled to find that he had died in Seattle, Washington in 1889. When did he return to the West and why?[17]

I discovered he had a hotel in Woodstock, Maine from 1856-1862. His daughter, Sarah Weston, worked there and she met a fellow employee, John Dibblee. They were married in 1862. Two years later the couple traveled to Dutch Flat in the California gold country where Sarah Dibblee worked for her brother, Nathan, in his sawmill. In 1869 she and her husband relocated

to Rainier, Oregon where her uncle, Dean Blanchard, was living.

Another of Nathan's sisters, Mary, had also traveled to the northwest and married John Leery of Seattle, Washington. It was to their home Merrill came, and where he died in 1889 at the age of eighty-five.

In 1881, my Aunt Sarah, age twelve, came to Seattle and also lived in the Leery home while she completed her one year

Students and a few of the faculty of the Territorial University of Washington, 1883. Sarah Blanchard attended this school two years earlier, in 1881.
Courtesy University of Washington Libraries, Special Collections (UW 2227).

of formal schooling at Territorial University of Washington. While there she took painting classes, which she later continued in San Francisco.[18]

---

[17] There are two letters from Merrill to his son, NWB, in the Blanchard Collection at the Museum of Ventura County. Neither gave me the information I was seeking. The first, dated May 1867, shows him still to be in Maine. The second, dated March 1869, is postmarked Rainier, Oregon where his brother, Dean, was living. Both letters tell of continued financial difficulties. Great great-grandfather Merrill did not appear to have the Midas touch!

---

[18] The above information on Merrill Blanchard was gleaned from Dean Blanchard, *Of California's First Citrus Empire* (1983).

Great Grandfather's Luck Begins to Change

MEANWHILE, NATHAN'S CONNECTION with Jno. Kneeland took him from Tennessee Gulch to Independence Hill, Mono Flat, Iowa Hill, Wisconsin Hill and finally, in 1858, to Dutch Flat. He was not without longings for home. In May 1857 he wrote, "Anxious as I am to get away from California, either to renew my studies or perhaps to go into some business…." But he resolved to stay and work even harder.

Such enterprise was noticed and rewarded, as he was elected collector in the district in which he lived in 1862, and in 1863 he was elected to the State Assembly for one term. He served on the Committee of Education and was the author of a bill that was always a favorite bit of family history for my brothers and me, which, "…suppressed vice and immorality prevalent in the mining camps… especially the bands of girls who periodically visited the mining communities, dancing and playing the tambourine and making the saloons their headquarters."[19] The bill passed.

Great grandfather was a staunch Congregationalist all his life, helping to establish the Congregational Church in Saticoy, predecessor of today's Church of the Foothills, where I am now a

---

[19] *American Families: Genealogical and Biographical from Most Authentic Sources*, 55.

NWB about the time of his marriage to Ann Elizabeth Hobbs in 1864.

NWB looking very grand in his Knight's Templar regalia. He also was invested as Worshipful Master of the Blue Lodge Masons while living in Dutch Flat. He continued both affiliations after relocating to Southern California.

member. He also supported the Methodists, donating the land in Santa Paula where the Methodist Church congregated for many years.

He became a Mason during these years and was affiliated with the Independent Order of Odd Fellows for more than fifty years, going through many levels of fraternal leadership in both organizations.

In 1863, Nathan undertook the next great chapter in his life, although I doubt he realized it at the time. (Only in retrospect do we have the perspective to note such demarcations.) He left Dutch Flat and traveled down the state at the invitation of his first cousin, Jotham Bixby, in Long Beach. It was during that trek Nathan first saw the Santa Clara Valley where he eventually would make his home and his fortune.

Bixby, also from Maine, had come 'round the Horn in 1852, and was considered the "Father of Long Beach" and an early agricultural pioneer, experimenting with citrus as well as raising livestock. He commissioned his cousin to, of all things, drive a herd of sheep to the railhead in St. Louis. From there Nathan went on to Maine to reconnect with his family.

This chapter of great-grandfather's life always posed a conundrum to me. Although I believed the story to be true, it made no sense. A sheep drive east to St. Louis in the middle of the Civil War—really?

I have later discovered that such a drive was indeed plausible and happened not in spite of the Civil War, but because of it. Sheep raising, like many enterprises in the United States, had been moving west since the 1830s. It cost one to two dollars per head to raise a sheep in the East, but only twenty-five cents to a dollar to raise one on the free land and wide-open spaces of the West.[20]

---

[20] L.G. Connor, "A Brief History of the Sheep Industry in the United States." *Agricultural History Society Papers* (1921).

Jotham Bixby was NWB's cousin who had come from Maine to California around the Horn of South America in 1852. The two men had much in common including early citrus and livestock production and community building. Blanchard was known as the Father of Santa Paula and Bixby, the Father of Long Beach. Bixby was to provide an essential lifeline to Blanchard who experienced near-financial ruin in 1880. The two men would both die in 1917.

With the advent of the Gold Rush in California and other rushes in Utah and Colorado, the demand for mutton was high. Wool was usually just

Rams for Sale.

THE UNDERSIGNED have two hundred American or Spanish Merino Rams, selected from the well-known stock of Flint, Bixby & Co. For sale at their place in Santa Paula.

July 3, 1875.
11-1m   BLANCHARD & BRADLEY.

NWB with his silent partner, E. L Bradley, undertook raising sheep and growing alfalfa when Blanchard first moved to Santa Paula. Advertisement in the *Ventura Signal,* July 3, 1875.

used locally, but the quality of wool-producing sheep greatly increased with the import of fine Merino sheep from the East and Europe.

The Honorable Charles Fernald was originally from North Berwick, Maine, where he met and married Hannah Hobbs, great-grandmother Ann Elizabeth's sister. They went west and he became sheriff of Santa Barbara County and later judge of the Court of Sessions from 1853-1861.

Then the advent of the Civil War disrupted the availability of cotton to produce uniforms, and so manufacturers turned to wool. Hence, young Nathan was likely taking valuable wool-bearing sheep to the railhead in St. Louis as part of the war effort.

Therefore a story that seemed nonsensical was, in fact, rooted in a shrewd business venture by cousin Jotham. Bixby again would appear in the Blanchard saga almost twenty years later.

After serving in the California State Assembly earlier in the year, Nathan arrived back in Maine in the fall of 1863, but instead of taking up a teaching career, resolved to return to California. Evidently other forces were at work. His cousin, Thomas Weston of Portland, Maine, wanted to introduce him to Miss Ann Elizabeth Hobbs of North Berwick, and came up with a plan. Nathan would be passing through North Berwick on an afternoon train, and Miss Hobbs was to meet him and give him a package to deliver to her sister, Hannah, wife of Judge Charles Fernald, living in Santa Barbara.

What follows is an account of that first meeting by my Aunt Sarah, Ann Elizabeth Hobbs' daughter.

> Mother performed this commitment none too willingly. There were other appointments for the afternoon; she was glad of the opportunity to send a parcel to her sister, but why couldn't this tiresome man just as well have chosen some other day to be coming through? Someone's horse and buggy had to be borrowed to carry her to the depot and altogether, it was just a mess, and the man was nothing but a nuisance! This was the spirit in which she drove to the station![21]

She must have changed her mind about the tiresome man, for they soon became engaged. Nathan wanted to marry and bring his bride back with him to California, but Ann Elizabeth hesitated. California was a long way off and in North Berwick and Portsmouth, a large circle of friends and relationships enlivened the residence of her uncle, Ichabod Goodwin, the governor of New Hampshire. Here follows another gem of description by Aunt Sarah,

> There gayety abounded in the persons of four girls whom I grew up to know as Cousin Abbie, Cousin Hope, Cousin Susie and Cousin Georgette.

> The story of this household of merry, fun-loving girls is a trifle unusual. Cousin Hope never married; but the next three married Army and Navy men. Cousin Abbie Goodwin married D.E. Winder, an Army doctor.[22] Early in the marriage, she would come home to visit for a perfectly plausible reason, and then never again joined her husband until she went out West to be with him in his final illness. Every week they wrote to each other all through the years, and she always kept her husband's most recent letter in her pocket until replaced by a new one. The remaining two sisters died. Susie

---

[21] Sarah Eliot Blanchard, *Memories of a Child's Early California Days* (1961), 4.

[22] Ann Elizabeth and Nathan would visit Cousin Abbie Goodwin and D.E. Winder on their honeymoon in California.

was Admiral George Dewey's first wife. I do not recall the surname of Georgette's husband, but each, as her husband was called to distant assignments, retraced her steps to the Goodwin hearth with a baby, and, as the young mothers died, the children were brought up by Cousin Abbie and Cousin Hope.

To leave these surroundings, which had been the only life she had shared, was a terrifying outlook for my mother, and she told my father that she wanted the opportunity to consider it; if she found after he had gone that she could live without him, why, that would be the answer. If, on the other hand, she could turn her back on it all, she would voyage to California....[23]

All this reads like a version of *Little Women*, but these remarkable women were very real. In an extraordinary and deeply poignant postscript Sarah writes,

It was indeed a leap into the dark she was about to make. At the engagement, it had been agreed that Mother was to go back in five years to see her mother, but more than twenty-five years elapsed before she returned to North Berwick, and her mother had long since died....

Ann Elizabeth traveled around the Horn of South America accompanied by her brother, Hiram, and his wife, Fanny, to be married in San Francisco. She packed a trunk full of household items that were hard to get in California and set sail, lamenting that she had not heard from "Mr. Blanchard" for almost two months. "I think California is the most discouraging place to write to...."[24]

Great-grandfather was fretting, too. He had sold his butchering enterprise, also the ranch in Santa Clara he had purchased from his father, plus some

Great grandmother Ann Elizabeth Hobbs of North Berwick, Maine during the early years of her marriage.

other pieces of property, and had bought a sawmill, but that was not to begin until the spring...and so he waited.

Ann Elizabeth finally arrived and the two were married in December 1864 at the Lick House in San Francisco, the leading hotel of the period. They went to Black Point, in Marin county, on their wedding trip, where Ann Elizabeth's cousin, Abbie, and her husband, D.E. Winder, were stationed. He was the garrison doctor. (This was the couple who would later separate, she returning home to New Hampshire, and they then corresponded weekly for the duration of their marriage. Certainly a strange arrangement, but evidently one that worked for the two of them.)

After the wedding they went to Dutch Flat, a thriving mining town, but during their first summer they lived in a lumber camp where Ann Elizabeth remembered she felt alone, isolated and bereft of female company. Once, when her husband had

[23] Sarah Eliot Blanchard, *Memories*, 4-5.

[24] *Ibid.*, 6. They referred to each other this formally until the advent of children when they called each other Mother and Father.

NWB about 1870 looking dapper and prosperous.

been gone all day and she was feeling particularly forlorn and neglected, she lay in bed crying when the Chinese cook tapped on her door, and when she didn't answer, peeked into the room and sized up the situation at a glance. He assured her that her husband was, "…a heap good man," and pointing a finger to her best bonnet—which dangled up in the rafters, to be dropped down by means of a pitch fork when needed—went on to assure her that, in due time there would be "lots of hats, lots of clothes, lots of everything!"[25]

What a shock this new life must have been for a cultured and carefree young woman. According to Aunt Sarah, her mother was an insatiable letter writer and kept her friends and family back home up to date with tales of her new life which, although very real and often grim to her, probably sounded exciting and romantic to them.

_____
[25] Sarah Eliot Blanchard, *Memories*, 7.

Their letters, in return, were avidly shared with the California family to the extent that when Sarah went east for the first time when she was twenty, she found she knew her cousins and how they all related to one another as well as they knew themselves because, "I had dwelt since infancy with every one of them!"[26]

Reading my great-aunt's book, *Memories of a Child's Early California Days*, serves as a remarkable testament to the education she and her siblings received from their mother. The book is charming, wonderfully descriptive, and altogether beautifully written, and this by a person who received only one year of formal education.

Meanwhile, the lives of Nathan and Ann Elizabeth progressed in Dutch Flat, punctuated by the arrival of three children, Dean Hobbs born in 1865, Sarah Eliot in 1868 and Eunice Weston in 1871, and Nathan's increasing business success.

In 1865, Nathan revisited the Santa Clara Valley, this time accompanied by his business associate, Elisha L. Bradley, an affluent owner of mining properties in Placer County and later a senator from Plumas County. They rode from Ventura to Newhall and marveled at the expanse of mustard-studded land with, "not an animal to fatten on it."[27]

It is very likely the two stopped at Rancho Camulos on their way through the valley and saw the successful orange orchard planted by Don Antonio del Valle a decade before.

In the Santa Paula area they passed through, George G. Briggs had bought a substantial portion

_____
[26] *Ibid.*, 8.

[27] "The Narrative of Jefferson Crane: As Told to E.M. Sheridan in 1921," Ventura County Historical Society *Quarterly* (February 1956). The reason for this absence of livestock was that the winter of 1863-64 was so dry no grass germinated. "As a consequence 90% of all domestic animals of the county died of starvation."

  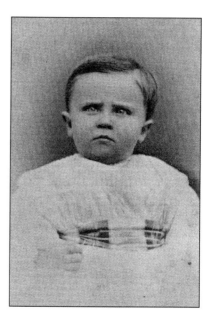

The Children of NWB and Ann Elizabeth (L-R): Sarah Eliot, Eunice Weston, and Nathan Weston, Jr. The girls were born in Dutch Flat and Nathan was born in Santa Paula, shortly after the family moved there in 1872.

of the 17,773-acre Mexican land grant Rancho Santa Paula y Saticoy in 1862 from T. Wallace More and his brothers, who in turn had bought it from the original grantee, Manuel Jimeno Casarin.[28] Briggs, a forty-niner, had made money growing produce for the mining camps. A successful orchardist from Marysville, he intended to grow and sell produce from this choice property between Ventura and Santa Paula Creek and capture the early market in San Francisco. In conjunction with Elijah B. Higgins in 1867, the property was subdivided into 150-acre tracts. A section east of Fagan Barranca was set aside as a townsite and lots of ten and twenty acres were laid out.

The great drought of 1863-1865 ruined Briggs and the untimely death of his wife further shattered the man. He left the valley forever. Higgins meanwhile, along with E.S. Wooley, surveyed and installed a water diversion system. "The upper ditch delivered water for irrigation lands along the westerly side of Santa Paula Canyon, mill operation and domestic water use for the (soon-to-be) town of Santa Paula. The lower ditch delivered water for irrigation of lands in Santa Paula Canyon and lands located on the valley floor between Ojai Road and Fagan Canyon."[29]

In 1871, Higgins built and put into operation a water-powered mill for grinding grists, and called it Santa Paula Mill.

Mill grinding stone.

[28] Robert M. Clarke, "The Beginning of the Briggs District," *Narrative of a Native* (1936), 134.

[29] Vernon Freeman, *People-Land-Water: Santa Clara Valley and Oxnard Plain, Ventura County, California* (1968), 11.

BODY MISSING 65 YEARS FOUND AT DUTCH FLAT

Dutch Flat, April 21.—The mystery of the disappearance of a body from the grave wherein it was placed, an incident which deeply stirred the Dutch Flat of 65 years ago, was partly cleared this week by the finding of the metal casket containing the body. Why the body, that of a child, was abstracted from

According to William Bellows, 8 is probably a 5-year-old infant nam five years ago, whose remains myst

A Death and a Birth: Origins of Santa Paula

BUT LET US RETURN TO DUTCH FLAT and the lives of my great-grandparents. Nathan's business ventures, especially the sawmill, were very profitable and the future looked bright. Then, in 1871, tragedy struck. Little Dean Hobbs Blanchard died of a mysterious brain malady and his parents were grief-stricken by the loss. According to Aunt Sarah, "…this may have been the reason they decided to leave Dutch Flat and come to Southern California."[30]

What ensued was a strange mystery that would not be solved until sixty-five years later. The little body was interred in a bronze coffin, unusual at the time, but the plan was that once the family was resettled in Santa Paula, it would be shipped to them. After living ten years in the Santa Clara Valley, the Blanchards arranged for the grave to be opened, but there was no coffin. Evidently the doctor who had attended little Dean's last days at the time was rumored to have robbed the grave in order to do a post-mortem. His parents were devastated anew,

Little Dean Hobbs was the first born of NWB and Ann Elizabeth. He died of a mysterious brain disease in 1871. His grave was robbed and the location of the tiny body was not discovered until 65 years later.

but put a marker with his name and obituary dates in the Santa Paula Cemetery.

In 1933, Sarah was forwarded an article from the *Sacramento Bee,* which contained a statement by G.E. Sharon, deputy coroner of Dutch Flat. After reading the coroner's account, she felt positive that the body of little Dean had been located. A bronze coffin had been unearthed in a local orchard. The remains were unimpaired except for the skull, which had been broken into four or five pieces. She felt that any accident of this sort in the horse

---

[30] Sarah Eliot Blanchard, *Memories*, 9.

and buggy days would have been remembered and talked about and she would have heard her parents discuss it. "So at last the body of their dear child was brought to Santa Paula and put in the family cemetery where they had wished it to be."[31]

When Nathan Blanchard and his family moved into the area in April of 1872, he bought 2,700 acres of the Briggs subdivision with Higgins. Included in the purchase were both the townsite and the water rights to Santa Paula Creek. He then bought out Higgins' half and sold it in October of 1872 to his associate in Dutch Flat, Elisha L. Bradley. Known as Blanchard & Bradley, it was a partnership of equal investment. They began by raising sheep and alfalfa. Mr. Bradley remained in Northern California as a silent partner, "depending on Mr. Blanchard's shrewdness and enterprise to invest the partnership's funds."[32]

Blanchard soon recognized the potential for building and operating a flour mill. Grain was rapidly being planted in Simi Valley and Ojai and the need for such a mill was increasing. The Blanchard & Bradley partnership owned water rights and the site of Higgins' old mill, which was opened as the Santa Paula Flour Mill in the spring of 1873. At the time it was the only flour mill between Los Angeles and San Luis Obispo.

> Soon bags of the mill's products appeared on the shelves of dry goods stores throughout the county. The first grade brand, 'Middlings Purified' was of such high quality that a bag shipped to the Nation's Centennial Exhibition in Philadelphia in 1876 was awarded a gold medal.[33]

In 1874, Santa Barbara nurseryman Dana B. Clark selected Santa Paula as the site to experiment with growing semi-tropical fruit. He partnered with Blanchard & Bradley early in 1874 and planted 100 acres of Havana Seedling oranges. (Later, forty acres would be budded over to lemons.) The partnership would provide the land and water, and Clark would plant and take care of the trees.

An article in the *Ventura Signal* in March 1874, touted the event:

> The planting out of the big orange orchard in the Santa Paula Valley has attracted much attention to that delightful section of country, and many are already talking of trying to get homes there. The little town of Santa Paula has a bright future, and it will not be many years before the great anticipation of its citizens will be realized.

Blanchard & Bradley controlled water both for irrigation and domestic uses. They had the original townsite expanded and surveyed and the plat map was recorded in June of 1875. As a result, more families moved to Santa Paula.

In 1873 there were estimated to be sixty families or about 210-250 people living in Santa Paula. Two decades later that number had grown to 1,000.[34]

Clark was originally contracted to care for the citrus orchard for ten years, but was soon in financial trouble. By 1877, Blanchard & Bradley were the sole owners of the property. Blanchard had high hopes for the orchard, but in fact it would be fourteen years, in 1888, before it came into production. A very good thing, because in that same year, a fire of unknown origins destroyed the mill that had certainly sustained the family during all these years.

---

[31] Sarah Eliot Blanchard, *Memories*, 10.
[32] Mary Alice Orcutt Henderson, *The History of Santa Paula, From Metates to Macadam, Prehistoric Times to 1917* (1980), 2.
[33] *Ibid.*

---

[34] Dean Blanchard, *Of California's First Citrus Empire*, 94.

1875 newspaper advertisement for flour from the Blanchard & Bradley Mill in Santa Paula. The mill was the only one between Los Angeles and San Luis Obispo and the quality of the flour was excellent. A bag of Midlings Purified received a gold medal from the Nation's Centennial Exhibition in Philadelphia in 1876.

BELOW: lithograph of the mill and farm buildings, with the Blanchard family home and orchards (inset), from *History of Santa Barbara & Ventura Counties* (Thompson & West, 1883).

ORANGE ORCHARD, MILL & FARM BUILDINGS OF BLANCHARD & BRADLEY, SANTA PAULA, VENTURA CO. CALIFORNIA.

A Death and a Birth: Origins of Santa Paula **71**

Early depiction of NWB's orange orchard planted in 1874. This image serves as the endpapers of this book and was previously used in books written by Aunt Sarah and my uncle, Dean Blanchard. (Thompson & West, *History of Santa Barbara & Ventura Counties*, 1883.)

A photo of the Blanchard & Bradley Mill, on the northeastern edge of Santa Paula, is less impressive than the engraving.

In 1880, a quirky tragedy upended the rising fortunes of the Blanchards of Santa Paula. Elisha Bradley, Nathan's silent partner all these years, was bitten by a cat. Within three weeks gangrene had set in and he died. He left no will. It is tempting to speculate if events would have turned out differently if there had been a will in place.

The early Blanchard & Bradley partnership had been a fifty-fifty split, but in the almost decade that followed, Blanchard had borrowed heavily to develop the property. As a result, he now owned only one-sixth of the investment.

Enter a figure who was known in family lore only as "The Widow Bradley."[35]

The Widow sued to recoup her share of the partnership. She was awarded 2,250 acres, not only the property on which the mill was located, but also the land on which stood the Blanchard family's home. The Blanchards were left with the half interest in the water company and 450 acres that included the non-producing orange and lemon orchard.

The family was thrust into turmoil. Ann Elizabeth, Eunice and Nathan Jr. (who had been born in Santa Paula in 1873) went to live in Santa Barbara with their aunt, Hannah Fernald. Sarah, almost fourteen, was invited to live with the George C. Sewell family, whose ranch bordered their property.[36]

Nathan, meanwhile, was virtually penniless. Said Aunt Sarah, "Had it not been for the generosity of his cousin Jotham Bixby who lent him $5,000, it would have been as dark a picture as that of any slum dweller."[37]

In 1880, NWB's partner, E.L. Bradley, died unexpectedly. Bradley's widow sued to regain her share of the partnership, leaving the Blanchards the non-producing orange orchard and the foreman's residence into which they moved.

Jotham's loan was a truly magnanimous lifeline; equivalent to more than $125,000 in today's dollars.

The family eventually moved into the former ranch foreman's house that was on their remaining piece of property. According to Sarah, it would have been cheaper to build a new house than remodel this one, but her mother had a nostalgic attachment to the old house, and that somehow the move would not seem so drastic. Through the years, that home was gradually transformed into the beautiful *El Naranjal* of my youth.[38]

Nevertheless, the family practiced rigid economies. Honey substituted for sugar and their only meat was bacon or salt pork. "We children habitually scoured the neighborhood to hunt for discarded medicine bottles to wash and scald and sell to the drug store in order to bolster family resources," said Sarah. Fortunately, the family received regular care packages from the Goodwin cousins in New Hampshire, and that was how the children were clothed.

[35] In fact, her name was Ellen Mary Bradley. She died on June 20, 1885, soon after wreaking havoc on the Blanchards.

[36] Sarah Eliot Blanchard, *Memories*, 42.

[37] *Ibid.*

[38] According to historian Margo McBane, before the Southern Pacific Railroad came into Santa Paula in 1887, building or remodeling would both have been expensive. All materials would have been sent by train to Newhall and then brought by wagon across the valley to Santa Paula.

I love this image, probably taken in the mid-1890s, as it shows the elegant Queen Anne-style coach barn next to the still rather humble Blanchard home.

This early image shows *El Naranjal* beginning to look like the lovely home of Aunt Sarah that I knew as a girl.

The Santa Paula Academy was founded by NWB and other city fathers in 1887 as a "feeder" school for Pomona College. It became the Santa Paula High School in 1891.

Starting over at almost fifty could not have been easy for Nathan and his family, and yet he appeared to have rebounded rather quickly from the shocking events of 1880. Even during the fragile recovery years, he and great-grandmother contributed to many charities, and in 1887, helped to establish the Santa Paula Academy.

The school, with close ties to the Congregational Church, was envisioned as a "feeder" to Pomona College, which Nathan had participated in founding in 1886. State laws mandated against religious affiliation in public high schools, so in 1891, the Academy became the Santa Paula Union High School.

NWB continued his affiliation with Pomona for the rest of his life. At his death in 1917, an obituary written by Charles B. Sumner, who oversaw the business and financial management of the college from its inception, included the following,

> Mr. Blanchard was present at the first meeting of the board…The trustees elected Mr. Blanchard

Vice-President of the board and for ten years he responded to the call of the college in some capacity nearly every month, although as the trains ran, it cost him two days at least at every call. During this time he gave freely of his time, his thought and his money, and equally of his credit which was quite as necessary.

Mr. Blanchard will always be particularly remembered for his foresight and generosity in purchasing and providing for the care of the grounds lying east of the college campus. This tract of sixty acres of oak and other native trees is not only a great addition to the attractions of Claremont, but an asset of fine civic and educational value. In naming this noble forest land Blanchard Park the college has established a living memorial of one who desired that nature as well as art should have a worthy share in the education of youth.[39]

Blanchard Park, or "The Wash" as it became known, still serves that purpose at Pomona College today.

---

[39] Dean Blanchard, *Of California's First Citrus Empire,* 187-188.

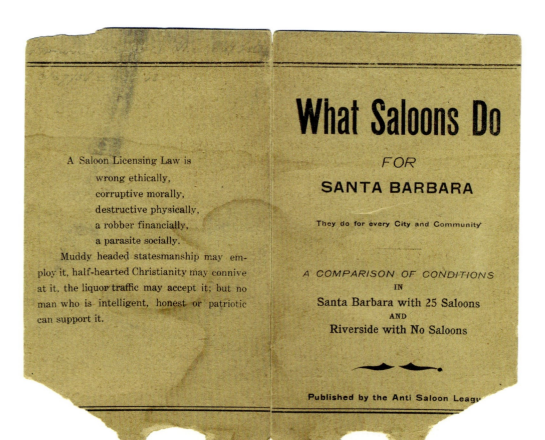

What Saloons Do

FOR
SANTA BARBARA

They do for every City and Community

A COMPARISON OF CONDITIONS
IN
Santa Barbara with 25 Saloons
AND
Riverside with No Saloons

Published by the Anti Saloon Leagu

A Saloon Licensing Law is
wrong ethically,
corruptive morally,
destructive physically,
a robber financially,
a parasite socially.

Muddy headed statesmanship may employ it, half-hearted Christianity may connive at it, the liquor traffic may accept it; but no man who is intelligent, honest or patriotic can support it.

For the year 1904	S. Barbara	Riverside	What Santa Barbara Gains from 25 Saloons
Population	11,000	11,000	
Assessed Valuation	$ 6,586,433.00	$7,019,905.00	
No. of Saloons	25	0	
No. of City Police	8	5	Expense of Three Officers
Total No. of Arrests	892	338	554 Arrests
No. of Arrests for Drunkenness	269	71	198 Drunkards
No. of Arrests for Dist. Peace	155	34	121 Rowdies
No. of Arrests for Vagrancy.	281	148	133 Tramps
No. Cases tried in Police Court	355	135	220 Police Court Trials
Received from Saloon Licenses	$7,500.00	0	$7,500. Blood money
City Tax Rate	1.30	1.10	Increased Tax Rate, $.20
Taxes Collected at above rate	$85.623.00	$77,218.00	Increased Taxes, $8,405.00
Deposited in Savings Banks	121,325.00	199,351.00	Loss in Savings, $78,026.00
No. of Churches (protestant)	9	21	Immorality and Crime
No. Scholars in Public Schools	1400	1898	Ignorance and Illiteracy
No. of Grocery Stores	16	19	Less Business
Meat Markets	5	8	Less Food
Stores	3	6	Less Comfort

Remnants of a pamphlet from the Anti-Saloon League comparing the crime rates of Riverside, with no saloons, to that of Santa Barbara with 25. My favorite line is the expense of "Blood Money"-$7,500 paid by the saloons for their licenses and, by inference, perhaps bribery? That I was able to find this amidst all the photographs and letters, was wonderfully fortunate and a tribute to the randomness of historical research.

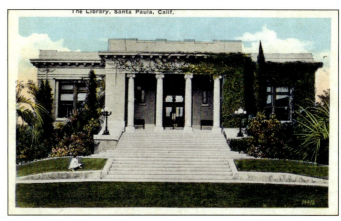

Postcard of the Dean Hobbs Blanchard Memorial library c. 1930. This gracious building was a gift from NWB and Ann Elizabeth to the City of Santa Paula in 1906 on the condition the town voted to go dry and not renew the licenses of the two remaining saloons. *Courtesy John Nichols.*

Dean Hobbs Blanchard Memorial Library

THE SANTA PAULA CULTURAL SCENE was also about to change. In 1906, the licenses of the town's two saloons expired. Great grandfather seized the opportunity and announced at a meeting in the Presbyterian Church, organized under the auspices of the Anti-Saloon League, "If Santa Paula goes dry, I will make a donation to the city." The licenses were not renewed, and Nathan Weston Blanchard was good to his word. The result of his $10,000 gift was the Dean Hobbs Blanchard Memorial Library. An article in the November 2, 1906 *Santa Paula Chronicle* said of the public meeting,

> Never before in the history of Santa Paula have so many people of different walks of life gotten together and become so interested in civic affairs...the meeting of October 28 must be set down as a red letter day, marking a new era of things civic.

Ground for the new building, designed by Los Angeles architect John C. Austin, was broken December 1908, and the interior finished in September 1909.

The library served the city until 1967, when it was declared unsafe. A new library opened at the end of 1969.

Another 1930s era postcard of the library showing its charming gardens. The old library was demolished in 1972. Like the razing of *El Naranjal* in 1966, this act of historical desecration makes me weep. *Courtesy John Nichols.*

The Dean Hobbs Blanchard Memorial Library in 1963.

I remember the chain of events that led to the choice of location for the new library. In November 1960, a spectacular fire erupted in the Safeway store on 8th Street, catty-corner from the old library. I saw the flames from the porch of our home on the hill, and listened to the gun-like reports of exploding cans of food.

The Blanchard Community Library today is the center of community activity, providing children's activities and meeting rooms for a variety of community groups. It is also the location of the Santa Paula Art Show, begun in 1937 by famed local artists Jessie and Cornelis Botke and Douglas Shively, artist and local banker. It is reported to be the first juried art show in California. *Photo by John Nichols.*

The old library, although a beloved icon, had in 1967 been deemed unsafe and too small to continue. Originally built to hold 4,000 books, it now contained over 50,000. The Safeway had been gutted by the fire, but was structurally sound, and it was decided it would become the home of a new library. By 1969, the remodeled building was finished and ready for occupancy.

In order to move the books from one building to the other, community volunteers and boys from the high school physical education department formed a human chain and passed boxes of books in a line half-a-block long. The Friends of the Library baked 120-dozen cookies and Sunkist provided lemonade for the occasion.[40]

The opening of the new Dean Hobbs Blanchard Memorial Library was a gala affair. I stood with my family sipping champagne, when Eb Tate, a dear

family friend came up to my mother and said, "Elizabeth, did you see Sarah? She's over in Produce!"

And indeed she was. A portrait of Aunt Sarah hung on a wall of what would have been the Produce Section of the old Safeway.

But another historical tragedy awaited. In 1972, the beautiful old library was torn down. Although the property was sold to the Santa Paula Water Works and the proceeds used to build the current Community Center, to destroy that elegant building and more than half a century of history was an irreplaceable loss to our community.

The current Blanchard Community Library, now in its 110th year, has embarked on plans to expand and modernize as it continues to serve the community. And so the wrecking ball was stilled.

---

[40] *Santa Paula Chronicle*, November 11, 1969.

Disrupter—1893 Style

Santa Paulans turn out for the arrival of the Southern Pacific Railroad, which first came to town in 1887. *Photo courtesy Limoneira Archives.*

MEANWHILE, Blanchard's recalcitrant orchard finally began to produce. The timing could not have been better. In January 1887, the Southern Pacific Railroad came to Santa Paula and by 1890, the orchard was producing so prolifically that great-grandfather built a packing house adjacent to the tracks to handle the fruit. Not many years later, a spur line was laid to connect Limoneira.

On February 28, 1893, occurred another milestone in the life of Nathan Blanchard and the future of Santa Paula, the Limoneira Company was founded. The establishment of Limoneira in today's parlance would have been described as a disrupter.

At the end of the nineteenth century, most of the great Mexican land grants had been sold and subdivided. The major crops were dry land lima beans, wheat and barley, and the farms were mainly small family-owned operations.

As described by Tony Biasotti, in a *Pacific Coast Business Times* publication celebrating Limoneira's 125th anniversary, "The new company would grow a modern crop, with modern methods, on irrigat-ed land, and it would sell the products all over the United States."

As previously mentioned, the Southern Pacific Railroad came to Santa Paula in 1887, making it possible to ship goods coast to coast. "It was only then that an operation as big as Limoneira would be feasible."[41]

Limoneira was the vision of two very different businessmen, Nathan Weston Blanchard and Wallace Libby Hardison. Although both from Maine, they never knew one another prior to coming west. Blanchard, as we know, came to California during the Gold Rush, and Hardison in the state's first oil boom in 1883. Nathan Blanchard—at sixty-two—was a stern teetotaler and devout Christian, whereas Hardison, forty-three, was a restless entrepreneur, who, along with Lyman Stewart, also co-founded the Union Oil Company. Hardison left both business associates in 1896 to mine for gold in Peru.

---

[41] Tony Biasotti, *Limoneira Since 1893: Celebrating 125 Years of Agribusiness Success* (2018).

Workers at the N.W Blanchard Packing House located at the corner of what is now Main Street and Palm Avenue. This picture was taken October 13, 1895. Blanchard's original "boxing plant" was located up the hill at the ranch dormitory. Each lemon was hand wrapped with the label *El Naranjal* Lemons. *Photo courtesy Limoneira Archives.*

Wallace L. Hardison, as mentioned earlier, was an energetic, restless risk taker. Besides his starring roles in both the inception of the Union Oil Company of California (1890) and Limoneira (1893), he had a seemingly inexhaustible supply of talented nephews. Allen Crosby Hardison, a University of Maine-trained engineer, and Chester Brown would both join their great-uncle in Peru mining for gold.

Although A.C. Hardison and his son, Domingo, would be ac-

The two men had combined resources a year-and-a-half before Limoneira's founding to buy 413 acres west of Santa Paula for $60,000, and formed The Farmers' Irrigation Water Company to irrigate the land. The land was planted largely to lemons, but also with smaller acreages of oranges and walnuts.

In addition to Blanchard and Hardison, the others involved in the establishment of the company were Charles H. McKevett, John Irwin, Clarence Allyn, Allen Crosby Hardison, and Dr. Fred Salathe, all of whom were local investors and early Santa Paula boosters.

NWB joins his employees for this photo at the packing house. Note that he is sitting on a citrus crate. *Photo courtesy Limoneira Archives.*

Blanchard and Hardison proposed to the group that a corporation be formed that would buy the farmland and water company from Blanchard and Hardison, who would be the majority owners. The seven men agreed and among them raised $1 million to capitalize the company—equivalent to almost $29 million in 2020 dollars. (Limoneira's worth as a publicly-traded company in pre-Covid 2020 was about $460 million.)

tive in both the Southern California citrus industry and Limoneira, it was young Charles Collins Teague who came west at his great-uncle's invitation in 1893, at the age of twenty-two, who would figure most prominently in the Limoneira story.

His first job was pruning the eucalyptus windbreaks that marked the various orchard plots. He was paid a dollar a day, plus room and board. He

NWB in 1893 at the founding of the Limoneira Company.

Wallace Libbey Hardison, Limoneira co-founder; also co-founder of the Union Oil Co. of California.

Charles H. McKevett, first treasurer of Limoneira and active in many aspects of Santa Paula's growth, including the co-founding of the Santa Paula Academy and the development of one of the city's first planned neighborhoods, McKevett Heights.

Charles Collins Teague, general manager of Limoneira from 1898-1947 and responsible for major innovation within the Southern California citrus industry.

resolved to, "learn the lemon business from Mr. Blanchard." Teague went on to say, "To Mr. Blanchard is due the credit for developing much of the early knowledge and practice of citrus culture and to him I owe my first knowledge of the citrus business."[42]

[42] Charles Collins Teague, *Fifty Years a Rancher: The Recollections of Half a Century Devoted to the Citrus and Walnut Industries of California and to Forwarding the Cooperative Movement in Agriculture* (1944), 30.

In 1896, after three years learning the lemon business, young Teague was given control of his uncle's business operations when Hardison left for Peru. Hardison's investments were varied and included housing lots in Santa Paula and a three-quarter interest in the sprawling 5,200-acre Santa Paula Horse & Cattle Company, on which he built a race track located in the area of Telegraph Road and Haines Road.

C.C. Teague in 1903 in front of his stately home at 8th and Santa Paula Streets.

The home built by C.C. Teague which still stands today. *Photos this page and next courtesy Limoneira Archives.*

C.C. Teague became aware that his uncle was hugely over-extended and began to liquidate "around the margins" rather than cripple the core of his uncle's holdings. Among other things, the race track had to go. It was plowed under and planted to sugar beets.[43]

Wallace Libbey Hardison's larger-than-life existence was cut short in 1909, when he was killed at a railroad crossing in Roscoe near Sun Valley, Los Angeles. This tragedy is cruelly ironic as Eunice Blanchard Kelsey, her husband, Arthur, and their adopted son, Richard, would also perish in a railroad crossing accident in 1929.

When Hardison returned from Peru in 1898, Nathan Blanchard, age sixty-seven, was preparing to retire. The two decided to offer the job of general manager to C.C. Teague. Young Teague had already caught the attention of others in the burgeoning Southern California citrus industry. He was offered a ten percent interest in Limoneira in order to secure his services. C.C. Teague held the position of general manager until his retirement in 1947, when he was succeeded by his son, Milton Teague.

Although 1893 was in many ways a great time to launch the new endeavor, there followed a severe recession. The "Panic of '93" lasted for five years and was the worst recession until the Great Depression of the 1930s as banks failed, businesses and farms collapsed and unemployment was rampant.

Limoneira was very lucky to survive the 1890s. It was extremely capital intensive in the early years as its infrastructure was created, including the planting of 46,895 citrus trees, and building a packing house and worker housing.[44]

Additionally, as the orchards didn't come into full production until the early 1900s, row crops were planted to generate income. Plus, freezes in 1898 and 1899 killed three-quarters of the young lemons on the trees. The founders had to return to the original investors for additional cash, a practice that would continue until 1901.

Since Blanchard already had a producing orchard and a packing and distribution system, it was

---

[43] Dean Blanchard, *Of California's First Citrus Empire,* 169.

[44] Biasotti, *Limoneira Since 1893.*

December 1948 snow in Santa Paula! I have pictures of me all bundled up against the cold during this rare occurrence.

Lemons curing (turning from green to yellow) under canvas covers in the Limoneira packing house. This method of curing lemons was the invention of C.C. Teague, the foremost innovator in the California citrus industry. Teague's many innovations afforded Limoneira a remarkable competitive advantage in the burgeoning citrus industry.

agreed that the Nathan W. Blanchard Investment Company would buy and distribute all the fruit Limoneira would produce, which it did until 1897, when Limoneira began curing and shipping its own lemons. By January 1, 1896 Limoneira produced a modest 934 pounds of fruit, but between January 1, 1896 and January 1, 1897, the Limoneira tally soared to 96,700 pounds. All told, between August 1895 and April 1897, the aggregate weight totaled 190,629 pounds.[45]

That the young company became profitable in the early years of the new century was largely due to the management skills and innovative mind of C.C. Teague: he developed the first coal-burning orchard heaters; the first machines to wash citrus; the first connection with researchers at the University of California to find methods to fight pests and diseases. He pioneered the Teague Method for storing fresh citrus; putting fruit in open-walled areas instead of small rooms—the industry standard until the advent of refrigeration.

Teague also oversaw the first expansion of Limoneira. In 1907, it acquired the 2,300-acre Olivelands tract adjacent to the original property for $400,000 and in 1922, purchased the 550-acre Limoneira Del Mar property in Ventura for $400,000.

Nathan Blanchard also cast a long shadow. In 1913, at the age of eighty-two, he directed that all the seedling oranges on his home ranch in Santa Paula be budded to Valencias,[46] a move that would pay off handsomely in the 1950s when a boom in juice sales, especially for the new frozen orange juice, hit the country.

The company endured many problems through the years, including freezes and drought. One solution in 1896 was to create the Thermal Belt pumping station to raise water from the Santa Clara River. I have only to read a list of the water company boards my father served on in his role as both general manager of The Samuel Edwards Associates and a twenty-five-year member of the Limoneira board of directors to know the importance of water man-

[45] Dean Blanchard, *Of California's First Citrus Empire*, 103.

[46] Charles Collins Teague, *Fifty Years a Rancher*, 30.

agement. These included Santa Paula Water Works, Farmers Irrigation Company and the Thermal Belt Mutual Water Company.

Others problems included early onslaughts of aphids and Black Scale for which trees were covered in canvas tents and fumigated with hydrogen cyanide—imagine trying that today? In the 1950s the industry was plagued by Quick Decline, a virus borne by soil nematodes. All these are reminders today, as we face the challenge of the Huanglongbing (HLB) disease borne by the Asian Citrus Psyllid, that the agricultural industry is always facing one natural threat or another.

ABOVE: Trees tented and fumigated using hydrogen cyanide to control black scale. *Photos courtesy Limoneira Archives.*

LEFT: Early photo of Limoneira packing house showing the massive scope of the building.

First panoramic photo of Limoneira Olivelands property in 1907. *Courtesy Museum of Ventura County* (PN 37847).

Santa Paula has always loved a parade including this one circa 1920. *Photo courtesy Limoneira Archives.*

LIMONEIRA C
Santa

DORMITORY
ifornia

Wendell Dowling ©1992

I've had this 1992 etching by Wendell Dowling of the Limoneira headquarters in my office for many years. The building on the left was the original mens' dormitory and now houses the Limoneira administrative offices. Currently the building in the middle is a gracious public living room with a huge stone fireplace. The building on the right is the headquarters of Calavo Growers. For many years my Uncle Dean housed his eclectic collections from his world travels in the upper floor of the Calavo wing. The etching turns out to contain the names of individuals hidden in many spots in the work. A conversation with Wendell Dowling's widow, Lynne, confirmed the names of all of the artist's immediate family and grandchildren: Lynne, daughters Heather, Wendy and Laura and grandchildren Elizabeth, Rebecca, Jeff, Josh and Jeremy. Can you find these names? Hint: Rebecca, for instance, is located under tree at right.
Image by permission of Lynn Dowling.

C.C. Teague pictured here with a labor gang made up primarily of Chinese workers. Chinese made up the bulk of the Limoneira labor force during the 1890s and first years of the twentieth century.

Labor Challenges

LABOR HAS BEEN a sensitive and pervasive issue at Limoneira and for all of California agriculture. For instance, although the Limoneira Company offered housing, in the early days the quality of housing provided to Anglo workers, which included a swimming pool and single-lane bowling alley, was vastly superior to that provided for immigrant workers from China, Japan and Mexico.

Chinese laborers made up the bulk of the agricultural labor force during the 1870s and 1880s. Later, Japanese workers began to come into California and by 1908, about 100 Japanese laborers were employed at Limoneira.

> Between 1914 and 1919, 5,000 Mexicans came north to work in the California citrus industry, and many found their way to Santa Paula. This migration continued during the 1920s, and Mexicans ultimately came to be the predominate agricultural labor force.[47]

The system at Limoneira and other ranches in Ventura county, however, was paternalistic at best and, in reality, semi-feudal. Laborers were provided housing at reasonable rates, a company store at which to buy necessities and separate schools to

learn English. Wages were kept low and offered no way for a worker to advance within the system.

In 1941, laborers were officially paid thirty cents an hour, but took home substantially less. That same year the American Federation of Labor moved into Santa Paula and sought to organize the pickers. The growers resisted and 6,000 workers walked off the job. The growers, led by C.C. Teague, refused to

Latino labor came to be the norm on the ranch from about 1914 onward. *Photos this page courtesy Limoneira Archives.*

---

[47] Belknap, "The Era of the Lemon," 127.

Santa Paula Water Works et al v. Julio Peralta 1893

I have commented earlier on the policies of racial discrimination that characterized not only Santa Paula, but all of California, and indeed the whole country in the later years of the nineteenth century. One such incident involved court proceedings surrounding Julio Peralta and the property he owned adjacent to Santa Paula Creek. It is not my intention to conduct a learned review of the situation. I am not qualified to do so, but at the moment in history that I write this, our country is engulfed in the discussion of the role of the past as it informs present actions. I feel I need to present what I have discovered. The following information was taken from Martha Menchaca's book.

Peralta owned property along Santa Paula Creek that sustained his crops and livestock. In 1893, a court case was brought against him claiming he did not hold legal title to the land. (Santa Paula Water Works et al v. Julio Peralta 1893)

The Ventura County Superior Court ruled he did hold title to the land because he was a United States citizen of Spanish descent. This is an important point because as a person of "pure Spanish descent," he was deemed "white" and entitled to enjoy the rights of an American citizen. Mexicans of mixed Native American descent were not considered white and did not enjoy any such standing. That Peralta had the use of the water was ruled a moot issue as he had lived on the property that contained most of the creek for twenty-seven years.

In 1896, there was a shortage of water in the creek that the newly established Limoneira badly needed. Nathan Blanchard and the company appealed the 1893 decision to the State Supreme Court. (Santa Paula Water Works et al v. Julio Peralta 1896.)

Their attorneys, Orestes Orr and W.H. Wilde, contended Peralta had no legal right to use the water as he was a Mexican and a foreigner and as such had illegally used the water for twenty-seven years.

The State Supreme Court upheld the Ventura Superior Court decision and ruled that Peralta and the owners of the Limoneira Ranch must share the water. The judge, C. Britt, admonished the plaintiff's actions in the entire affair. He said no one in Santa Paula had the right to act as an immigration and naturalization agent. No one had the right to dispossess Peralta of his civil rights because they did not believe he was a citizen.

According to historian Mitch Stone, "The case wended its way through the courts until 1896, when Peralta was awarded only a fraction of the water he had earlier claimed. The costs of the lawsuit and its outcome left Peralta deeply in debt and with little hope of recovery, but for the Water Works the judicial victory finally secured the town's water supply." (*The Oaks of Santa Paula*, 2010.)

Did might make right in this situation? In my opinion, assuredly yes. Were the actions of the plaintiffs the product of their times? Again, I believe they were. Am I glad there is not a statue of Nathan Blanchard somewhere in town? Again, yes, because it would very likely be the focus of the type of discussion/dissent we are witnessing today.

The first dormitory was built about 1898 to house Anglo male workers.

pickers and their families set up tent camps and tried to continue their protests. One such camp in Steckle Park was dubbed "Teagueville."[48]

After six months, the strike collapsed and the pickers went back to work at the old low wages. Said C.C. Teague, "I am not opposed to organized labor, but I am unalterably opposed to exploitation of workers by irresponsible labor leaders."[49]

arbitrate and hired junior college students and Dust Bowl migrants to break the strike.

The growers played hardball and evicted the workers from ranch housing. The displaced

Single family housing circa 1920.

Women have always been the primary labor force in the packing house during most of Limoneira's history. They do not engage in field work.

Photos this page courtesy Limoneira Archives.

I recently spoke with Alfonso Guilin who started with the company in 1966 as labor relations manager.[50] He said that overtones from the 1941 strike lingered, with many of the older workers still harboring resentment against upper management. He said that the Dust Bowl migrants who had been brought in as strike breakers were now middle

---

[48] Martha Menchaca, *The Mexican Outsiders: A Community History of Marginalization and Discrimination* (2010).

[49] Belknap, "The Era of the Lemon," 128.

[50] Conversation with Alfonso Guilin, June 2020.

(*continued on page 94*)

Santa Paula's Palm Avenue which stretched from the railroad tracks north to *El Naranjal*. The Santa Paula Academy would be built in 1887 at the base of the hill on the right.

Irrigation pipe being unloaded at the Limoneira railroad spur. What would O.S.H.A. say today?

Limoneira mules doing the hard work of orchard clearing.

C.C. Teague (top left) sits atop a pyramid of lemon boxes circa 1900.

A display of Limoneira produce at the Ventura County Fair circa 1900.

Wagons full of lemons line up to load at the Limoneira railroad spur circa 1900.

The fat and shiny mules of Limoneira — a good job if you could get it!

The Limoneira general store circa 1920.

Ladies of the packing house circa 1930. The inscription says it all—Santa Paula, Lemon Capital of the World!

All photos courtesy Limoneira Archives.

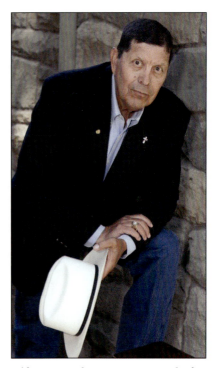

Alfonso Guilin came to work for Limoneira in 1966 as labor relations manager and retired as executive vice president in 1996.

SEATED L-R: Margie Smith, Essie Hillis, Ruby Jones, Pearl Shurley, Margarita Montanes, Francis Perez, Laverne Crow, Alberta Abbiatti, Jessie Garrett, Ada Morgan, Carmen Ayala, Edna Larkin, Drucilla Taylor, Margie West, Hazel Nowlin, Ruth Mullins, Mae Enke, Marie Cole, Perna White, Stella Moffett, FIRST ROW STDG.L-R: Ola Lewis, Odessa Sayre, Sadie Garner, Cirilo Perez, Ruel Garmon, J. R. Jones, Herb Locke, Homer Garrett, Nicholas Gonzales, Glen Davison, Raymond Griggs, Jack Garner, Allie Garner, Horace Enke, Leon Holloway, Homer Brenner, Burt Taylor, Robert Nowlin, Dewey Schwarting, Katherine Brown, Nellie Mejia. SECOND ROW STDG.L-R: Russell Best, Luther Cole, Lonnie West, Perley Randall, Lester Ross, Earl McKee, Clay Parker, Ernie Coy, Virgil Cole, Wm. Payne, Troy Gary, Eugene Tyler, Woodrow Garrett, Joe Larkin, Anton Woods, Elva Jenkins, Refugio Montanez. THIRD ROW: James Lewis, Homer Bryson, O. T. Haley, Montie Wells, Kenneth Olivier, Ted Morgan, Alan Polsson, Elvie Lindsey, Warner Brown, Delmer Spencer, Melvin Faulkner, Wm. Smith, E. Rodriguez, Jess Huskey, Mike Pinedo, Olen Morgan, Magdaleno Gonzales. FOURTH ROW: Wm. Mullins, Howard Abbiatti, Gus Quick, Fred Foote, John Crow, Wm. McKown, Ralph Lester, Oval Osburn, Clifford Manes, Sidney Taylor. TOP ROW: M. M. Teague, Jack McKinney, Leonard Cloonan, Wm. Goodman, Al Lang, Arch Moffett.

MARCH 9, 1969
EMPLOYEES OF LIMONEIRA COMPANY
WHO HAD COMPLETED 15 YEARS OR
MORE OF SERVICE.

A 1969 photo of employees retiring after fifteen years of service to the company.

managers. I asked whether there was resentment against them. He said no, as most workers lived on the ranch and their children played together, went to school together and many intermarried. The problem the Dust Bowl migrants had was prejudice from many people in Santa Paula who looked down on the "Arkies" and "Okies."

Al said that as the middle managers retired, they were largely replaced by Latino employees, and the Limoneira workforce today is predominately Latino.

My observation is that although several Latino men hold upper-level management positions, there have been no Latinos in top-tier management since Guilin retired in 1996 as executive vice president. There are also very few women in upper management. When queried, Al agreed with this characterization, but pointed out that it was not very different from the percentage of Latino and women in upper level management in the workforce at large. A true but not a very ringing endorsement for workplace equality.

Today, at the end of every annual meeting of Limoneira stockholders, pictures of the employees who had retired that year are displayed along with the number of years they worked for the company. It is rare to see someone retiring who has worked less than twenty-five years. In fact, many families have lived and worked on the ranch for generations. I think this speaks to the fact that Limoneira values its workforce who in turn finds it a good place to work, and in many cases, to raise their children and grandchildren.

Modern Limoneira

IN THE EARLY YEARS, both farm management and direction of the board of directors remained in the hands of the founders. That practice changed in 1967 when Volney (Bill) Craig became general manager, followed by Jack Dickenson and Pierre Tada. The chairmanship of the board of directors has remained in the hands of the founding families, exemplified today by the leadership of Gordon Kimball, a member of the Hardison clan.

Meanwhile the company has continued to grow. In 1986, The Samuel Edwards Associates' 1800-acre Orchard Farm was purchased. In 1994, the 500-acre Teague-McKevett Ranch east of Santa Paula was acquired. Today, it is the site of the Harvest at Limoneira's 1500-home housing development, the first homes of which were sold in 2019.

The approval process for the Harvest at Limoneira took over seventeen years and included a S.O.A.R special election that achieved an 83% favorable vote. This was perhaps not unexpected, but rather a vote of confidence in the company and its founders who through the years have built so many of Santa Paula's neighborhoods: in the 1920s McKevett Heights was developed; in 1960 the Blanchard Ranch extended housing on the western edge of town; in the 1970s and '80s the property on which the Santa Paula Hospital was built was

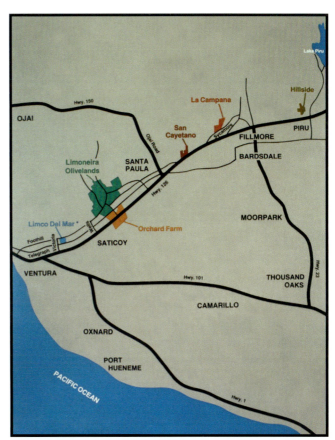

A map showing Limoneira properties in the Santa Clara Valley.

donated by the Teague-McKevett family who also developed neighboring hillside homes. The Harvest is an extension of the company's investment in the future of the city.

But perhaps the biggest change to take place at twenty-first century Limoneira occurred in 2004, when Harold Edwards was hired as president and CEO. Scion of the Samuel Edwards family, Harold changed the company's focus from local to global.

"When Harold came in it was such a breath of fresh air. We had never had someone with international experience, who really understood the wider world and its possibilities," said John Blanchard, former member of the board.[51]

---

[51] Biasotti, *Limoneira Since 1893*, 17.

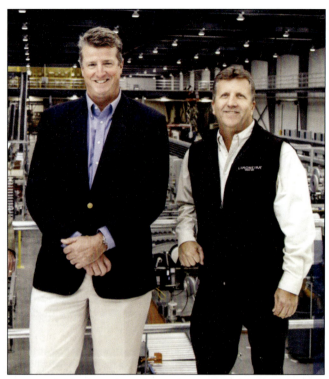

CEO Harold Edwards and VP of Farming Alex Teague, both scions of Limoneira legacy families, have led the company in new domestic and international directions.

"Sunkist is very production driven. Harold and I are very market driven," explained Alex Teague of the decision by Limoneira to assume its own marketing and distribution.[52]

Other changes occurred including the purchase of Windfall Farms, 750 acres of wine grape acreage in Paso Robles, plus other investments in the Central Valley, Mexico, Chile, Argentina and South Africa.

Such moves demonstrate the company's international focus. Under the slogan, *One World of Fresh Citrus,* this international presence gives Limoneira the opportunity to provide fruit year-round and world wide.

Another milestone in 2010 was the move to become a publicly traded company, a move required by the Securities and Exchange Commission because the company now had more than 500 shareholders.

Soon after Edwards hired Alex Teague, now senior VP of farming and COO, the great-grandson of C.C. Teague.

In 2010, the decision was made to separate from Sunkist Growers, the cooperative marketing and sales organization with whom the company had been affiliated for more than a century. This change was particularly significant as it was C.C. Teague, often called the father of collective citrus marketing, who had first joined the Southern California Fruit Exchange, which became Sunkist.

Logo for Limoneira's One World of Fresh Citrus initiative.

---

[52] Biasotti, *Limoneira Since 1893,* 18.

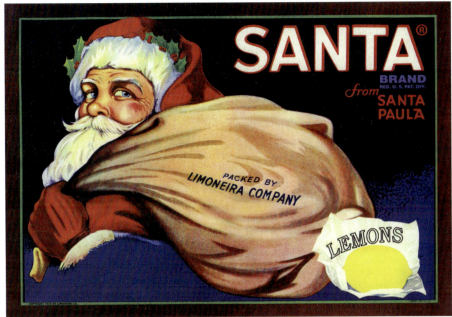

The iconic Santa citrus label designates the company's premium or fancy grade of fruit.

are replaced with younger trees, they are planted more densely, thus increasing yields using less land. The company has approximately 2 million trees that collective sequester approximately forty-eight million pounds (24,000 tons) of carbon annually. These assets coupled with organic waste recycling, solar energy and water savings projects are the very essence of sustainability. Said Alex Teague, "We're kicking back into gear what the founders would have

"We really weren't big enough to be publicly-traded from an efficiency of capital perspective, but our vision and our growth plans have put us in a place where it could be one of the greatest things to ever happen to us," said President and CEO Harold Edwards.[53]

In 2016, the company opened a new state-of-the-art packing house. Although employing the same footprint as the old facility, it has proved to be highly efficient and a direct boost to the bottom line.

In addition, the company is a leader in sustainable farming, which encompasses all aspects of operations including stewardship of both natural and human resources. For instance, Limoneira has over 15,700 acres of land and orchards. As older orchard blocks

The Paula label designates the second grade or choice fruit. Although the company still ships in cartons (cardboard, no longer wooden crates), the packing house is able to provide a wide array of packaging as dictated by customer demand.

wanted. They were risk takers. Their version of international then was New York, but in a smaller world I think they'd be doing exactly what we're doing."[54]

[53] Biasotti, *Limoneira Since 1893*, 19.

[54] *Ibid.*, 21.

I find it interesting to look over this catalogue of the changes and accomplishments at modern Limoneira or, in fact, what I have written of events at the ranch since the death of Nathan Blanchard in 1917. The reason is because these events were never front and center in my life. As a child the only thing about the company that really interested me was the fact that until the late '50s mules were still actively used on the ranch.

Although there were always two Blanchard representatives on the board of directors, including my father for the last twenty-five years of his life, and my brother John from 1970-2016, the goings on at Limoneira were distant and impersonal to me. Until Harold Edwards became president

A recent publication includes this page touting the company's dedication to sustainable farming.

and CEO in 2004, and began steering the company in a new direction, about the only personal contact I had was to attend the annual picnics and field days and to attend annual stockholder meetings.

All this would change in 2016 when my brother, John, retired from the board and I was elected to take his place...but more about that a bit further on.

Photo of the Limoneira work force taken on the occasion of the company's 125th anniversary.

Back to the Future

HMMM, LET'S SEE, when last I left off telling my story, I was feeling sad and disoriented: I had been shipped off to boarding school; Aunt Sarah, my father and grandfather had died; *El Naranjal* had been torn down; and the coach barn burned up. Did I also mention my beloved Jill dog had disappeared?

As I have previously written, the events of this time had a huge effect in shaping my life.

I have talked about a rocky start to my first year at USC in 1966, but fortunately I'm blessed with a resilient nature plus I had the backing of both family and the new friends I made at the Pi Beta Phi sorority. It was a fun time to be at USC. I was there when O.J. Simpson was a good guy! I thought going to the Rose Bowl every New Year's Day was what every college kid did.

Although many schools across the nation were caught up in protest over the Vietnam War, USC was largely quiet. This kind of non-involvement was to have repercussions later in my life, but at the time I let these events flow past me. I enjoyed my studies in modern European history and experienced an unforgettable summer in 1968, between my sophomore and junior years, on an archaeological dig in Israel.

How Much a Pound *are* Garbanzo Beans?

This was the summer after the historic June War[55] and an incredible time to be in Israel. With the spectacular defeat of the combined Arab forces in 1967, whole swaths of the country that had been closed off to Israelis since the formation of the country in 1948 were now recovered. These included: the Gaza Strip and the Sinai desert from Egypt; the Golan Heights from Syria; and the West Bank and East Jerusalem from Jordan.

I was part of a group of forty students from USC and Stanford led by two professors, Drs. Edward Phinney and Gerald Larue from USC. The trip had its origins two years earlier when a group of high-powered USC donors, led by industrialist Justin Dart, had gone to Israel and established valuable relationships with both government officials and some working-class Arabs who had been their guides and drivers.

As a result, the Israeli Department of Antiquities granted USC a permit to excavate a small "tell," or archaeological site, about an hour north of Jerusalem, thirty minutes south of the ruins of ancient Ceasaria, and about a mile east of the Mediterranean Ocean.

We stayed on a kibbutz called Nasholim, and each morning at dawn, before the heat became too intense, we marched out to the site, Khirbit Maz'ra, or "ruin of the planted field."

Israel's climate and topography are very like that of California and our small site, about a quarter-acre in size, rose twenty feet above the fields to the east and the road that bordered it on the west. The little tell was covered in chaparral and other familiar shrubs and was crowned with a large beehive.

Our leaders decided that a controlled burn was in order. We established our fire lines and set the site on fire. Unfortunately, the prevailing onshore breeze shifted off shore and the blaze jumped our fire lines and headed for the ocean, with all forty-plus of us frantically running after it. We soon had it out and were greatly relieved that the area burned seemed much like the tell itself, covered in dry shrubbery—nothing valuable.

Next morning, as we approached the site, we noticed a group of Arabs awaiting us, long robes and kufia head scarves fluttering in the breeze. How nice, we thought, that this contingent from a nearby Arab village had come to welcome us.

We soon discovered this was not a welcome party. The land our fire burned had, in fact, been planted in garbanzo beans and we had torched pretty much the whole crop. Our leaders hunkered down with the leaders from the village and a payment of $400 was negotiated. To this day I don't know if that amount represented a best-crop-year-ever or if we had narrowly averted an international incident. Later, I wrote about this in a very special class I was invited to join, presided over by Dr. John Hubbard, the president of USC from 1970-1980. I titled the paper, "How Much a Pound are Garbanzo Beans?" It was the first time I realized how history can reach forward though the ages and touch the present in a very real and visceral way.

We traveled to Jerusalem several times during that summer of 1968, and a small group of us, maybe six young men and women, made the acquaintance of the legendary Kando. He owned an antiquities shop across from the famous King David Hotel in East Jerusalem, and we had an *entre* thanks to the group of USC donors who had been there two years before.

---

[55] June 5-10, 1967.

Kando, a Christian Arab, was important because it was to him the Bedouin had brought the Dead Sea scrolls a decade-and-a-half earlier, and he, in turn, handled the presentation of the scrolls to the world. He was always gracious and welcomed us into his shop with tea and kind words. His *maître de*, so to speak, was a gentleman named Jusef Saud who had been the curator at the Rockefeller Museum in Jerusalem, but being an Arab, had lost his position after the June War.

Novices though we were, we quickly realized that not even experts could always distinguish between "real" antiquities and fakes. If we saw something in the shop we liked we would show it to Mr. Saud. If it was authentic he would nod and say, "Ah, very nice." If not he would nod and reply, "Ah, perhaps something else."

One day we arrived at the shop and went upstairs to Kando's office and found him assembling a necklace out of beads and amulets. I'll let good friend, John Orr, who was also a USC student and was there that day (and now a Ventura County lawyer) tell the story,

> I recall he made the necklace starting with a pendant piece of an alabaster lion. Then he would reach his hand into a large bag of beads and one by one a necklace emerged. When it was nearly completed he asked if I had a girlfriend who I could buy this necklace for and give to her. I demurred but I asked the price. He said $150.00. We dickered and his final ask was $60.00 and I didn't take it, thinking I would return and get it later.
>
> That night back at the kibbutz, the graduate student couple who helped lead the dig, told us they had been at Kando's late in the afternoon and Kando told them he had just obtained a Roman necklace and he would sell it for $600. They bargained and it was purchased for $500. It had an alabaster lion's head and many lovely beads. We who had watched Kando make it looked at one another... and congratulated the couple on their good fortune.[56]

The most memorable experience that summer was a visit to the ruins of Masada, the mountain fortress that rose from the floor of the Judean Desert overlooking the Dead Sea. From 73 to 74 CE, Roman troops besieged the fortress where 960 Jewish rebels had retreated at the end of first Jewish-Roman War. The siege ended with the mass suicide of every man, woman and child.

We climbed the steep path up to the mountain's plateau, leaving at three in the morning to escape the searing heat of the day. This was a time before the addition of trams that today whisk you to the top. Once at the summit, and just as the sun was rising, Dr. Phinney read from Josephus' heart-breaking account of the brave resistance and ultimate mass suicide. That day was one the most moving experiences of my life.

By the end of the summer, despite diligent excavations on our part, the little tell didn't yield much of value. In one area we unearthed evidence of a seventeenth century caravansary; in another a Crusader-era stable complex with lots of marvelous bits and other horse paraphernalia. The most interesting discovery was unearthing a beautiful Byzantine-era structure with an exquisite tiled floor. There was nothing the Israeli Department of Antiquities wanted for its own collections, so USC was allowed to bring home nearly five tons of pottery and other artifacts. I don't know what was ever done with them.

---

[56] Conversation with John Orr, September 2020.

Back to USC

RETURNING TO LIFE AT SC for my junior year was great fun. I met Jim Brown my freshman year and we had dated ever since. James Michael Brown was from a big, rambunctious, working class Catholic family from nearby Westchester. I loved his bright yellow VW bug, his surfing ability and the fact that Jim became Yell King, the leader of both men and women's cheerleading squads, and was definitely a "BMOC." I also admired the fact that although we came from very different backgrounds, he adapted to mine while never losing sight of his own, while I, hopefully, did the same. We married in 1969 at the end of my junior year.

We lived near campus while I finished my senior year, and in Woodland Hills as I completed my master's degree in modern European history. Jim, a born salesman, worked first for IBM and then became a stockbroker, a career he followed until his retirement. He trained in New York for several weeks and then we packed up and traveled around Europe for three months before moving back to Ventura County and Santa Paula in 1972.

We lived in a wonderful little house in that magical little enclave in Santa Paula called The Oaks, and I hadn't been in town long when I got a call from the late Mary Alice Orcutt Henderson, the modern version of "she who must be obeyed." Mary Alice, a

Jim Brown in USC yell leading uniform with his VW "Sunspot." How could a girl resist?

One of the best things about fraternity parties —always a great photographer on hand.

More fraternity party fun. I still have that wonderful "Twiggy" era dress.

Our official wedding photo that appeared on the front page of the *Santa Paula Chronicle* in June 1969. We honeymooned in Hawaii and returned the day Americans landed on the moon.

Pre-wedding photo in the garden of my childhood home. Photographer Robert Dana Teague had catalogued my life since I was six-months old.

Two of a kind! Jim Brown lights up the "cigar" of great family friend Fred Stewart at our cabin on Faria Beach in 1975.

respected local historian, was the daughter of early Union Oil geologist William Orcutt. She was the founder of the Santa Paula Historical Society and an energetic mainstay of the town's cultural life. She offered a menu of activities I could become involved with, and that's how I ended up leading a troop of Girl Scouts.

Next I joined the committee to celebrate Santa Paula's Centennial of 1875.[57] We had such a good time that the group stayed together to celebrate the 1776 Bicentennial. What a super gathering of active people: Mary Alice and her brother Bill, Angela Dominguez, and Jill Atmore to name but a few. We had a great time creating the Main Street Museum, where local store windows were filled with the memorabilia of Santa Paula's past. That group was the nucleus of the Santa Paula Historical Society.

---

[57] Although Nathan Blanchard had named and platted the town in 1873, the plat map was not recorded until 1875.

Life was awfully good. I joined the Assistance League of Ventura County, rode horses, and Jim and I played tennis at the Wilson tennis court in Santa Paula and later at Cabrillo Racquet Club. We traveled with good friends and in September of 1976, were blessed with the birth of Devon Elizabeth Brown.

About fifteen months later, Eliot Charles Brown arrived, but this sweet baby was born with only one lung and one kidney. We lost him when he was only eight months old.

Mom with little Eliot on her lap and Devon looking quizzically at the camera.

Earlier, I mentioned my mother's concern about "what people would think." I, however, need only to look in the mirror and see the same trait in myself. A painful example I so regret, was when little Eliot died of pneumonia. In those days parents were not allowed to stay in the room with their sick children. I arrived at Children's Hospital in Los Angeles to find that our darling boy had already died. I gazed at his still little form, his angel-blonde hair like a corona around his head, and realized that for the first time in his short life he was not struggling to breathe.

Jim arrived a few minutes later and burst into sobs. A nurse was in the room with us and I was embarrassed by his display of emotion. What must she be thinking, I wondered? In fact she was probably wondering why I hadn't done the same.

Another example of this emotional disconnect, and frankly a sign of my self-centeredness, occurred soon after as we prepared to leave the house for Little E's graveside service at the Santa Paula Cemetery, where he was laid to rest next to the grave of his great-great uncle, little Dean Hobbs. I was nervous and touchy and worried we would be late. Good grief, what were they going to do, start the service without us?

I regret that time and hope, now, forty-five years later, I have learned more humility, more compassion and more patience. I think tragedy of that sort can either bring a couple together or drive you apart. Unfortunately for Jim and me, it was the latter and we divorced in 1983.

Devon, age two, on the lawn of the Ebell Club after her first Santa Paula Halloween Parade.

For the next four years, Devon and I were on our own. I remember devising a list of things a single woman must learn to do by herself —two

of those were setting up her own Christmas tree and opening her own bottle of champagne. For me this was a challenging yet exciting time, but it was hard on Devon, who was seven at the time of our divorce. Although I was glad to be quit of Jim, he was a great dad and she felt his absence keenly. I am grateful the men I dated during that time were good and decent, providing loving male role models that never threatened her relationship with her father.

For me this was a time of discovery. I had segued from comfortable childhood to a comfortable college experience to a comfortable marriage without actively directing my course. I remember thinking that if making one's own decisions, good and bad, was the key to being a grownup, then I didn't really become a card-caring adult until I divorced at 35.

I wanted to see what I could do in the real world. I worked briefly in the development department of California Lutheran College and then went to work in public relations and marketing for the hybrid vegetable seed company Petoseed, where I honed my writing skills and learned about a different kind of agriculture. I also wrote about county business and agricultural history for various local and national publications.

The Next Chapter

THE NEXT CHAPTER OF MY LIFE opened in 1987, when I met and married the marvelous Richard Benjamin Chess, Jr. Dick was one of three brothers —Tom, Dick and Harry (Harry Ronald, called Ron), yes really! Dick graduated from Tufts University in 1957, and enlisted in the Marine Corps. From there he went to George Washington Law School. Upon graduation he went to work for, as he called it, "Bobby Kennedy's Justice Department."

Dick's first assignment was in Mississippi working on voter registration cases. Soon after he arrived in the capital, Jackson, he was invited to dinner at the home of the attorney general. Dick said he was greeted at the door by the attorney general's wife who glared at him and snarled, "What are youuuu doing down here?" Not a warm Southern welcome.

Dick then became part of history as one of the attorneys from the U.S. Department of Justice to accompany James Meredith as he sought to gain admission to the University of Mississippi in 1962. Dick described being part of a team that accompanied Meredith everywhere he went on campus. This consisted of Meredith in the lead, followed by two armed U.S. Marshalls behind him and behind them two attorneys from the Department of Justice, for two weeks Dick being one of them. On either side of this entourage were jeeps with six armed

Dick Chess and I enjoyed a honeymoon that included a New Year's Eve party in Paris in 1987. We were accompanied by six of our best friend couples!

soldiers travelling on parallel streets. "This was the configuration that went with him (Meredith) everywhere—to class, to the student union, to the library and home."

Dick and his first wife raised their family in Fairfax, Virginia, where he established a law firm. Dick loved playing golf and tennis and built the first indoor tennis club in the southeast. He became interested in real estate and that is what brought him to California where his brothers, Tom and Ron, both dentists, were living.

Dick and I met on a blind tennis date at the Pierpont Racquet Club in Ventura in July 1987, and were married the following December. We embarked on building our Ventura home three months after the wedding. Home building is always said to be hard on a marriage, but I recommend doing it as newlyweds when you are both so eager to please one another.

The following September I was presented with the opportunity to take over the Ventura County Farm Bureau publication, *The Broadcaster,* a job

In 1962, after graduating from George Washington Law School, Dick joined the Justice Department. One of his first assignments was to accompany James Meredith who was desegregating the University of Mississippi. Dick was not in this particular picture of Meredith being accompanied by soldiers and Justice Department attorneys, but his time on the job looked exactly like this. Marion S. Trikosko, photographer. *Courtesy Library of Congress, Prints & Photographs Div., Washington, D.C. (Item 2016646448).*

The Chess brothers, Tom, Dick and Harry. In this photo Harry Ronald, called Ron, is on the left with Dick in the middle and Tom on the right.

Richard Benjamin Chess, Jr. 1935-2013.

I loved for the next twenty-five years. In 2004, I changed the publication's name to *Central Coast Farm & Ranch* because broadcasting had lost its agricultural association, and for most people it meant something about radio and TV.

In 1989, I started down an equally challenging and fulfilling road. Dick was the president of the Ventura County Symphony and, inevitably, I became involved, first with its Design House project, then as president of the Symphony League. In 1995, the Ventura County Symphony and the Conejo Symphony Orchestra merged to become the New West Symphony. I even have the honor of having chosen the name. I served on the inaugural board and then, in 1997, was hired as executive director. I had a background in marketing and fundraising and I was a good team builder, but didn't know a thing about running a symphony. The first person I hired was an old symphony hand named Jim Reeves and from then on we hired people who were good at doing what we weren't. It was an exciting, nerve-wracking time, but today the New West Symphony is a flagship of county culture.

I left New West in 2002 and became the interim director for the Rubicon Theatre in Ventura, tasked with hiring the company's first full-time director. I next worked with Jordan and Sandra Laby's San Buenaventura Foundation for the Arts in an attempt to build a performing arts center in Ventura. The 2008 Recession quashed those hopes, but it provided me an opportunity to work with most of the performing and visual arts organizations in the county. During these years I was also on the founding board of Casa Pacifica and on the fine arts committee of the Museum of Ventura County.

My association with the museum was long and included the time my mother was president of the Docent Council and then president of the museum

People

New growth to tend

Betsy Blanchard Chess, whose great-grandfather helped establish the town of Santa Paula, tends a mandevilla at her Ventura home. She'll have more time for gardening when she leaves her post as executive director of the New West Symphony this week.

Michelle Yee / Special to The Star

Betsy Chess moves on after helping New West Symphony take root in county

August 27, 2002 article about my retirement from New West Symphony appeared in the *Ventura County Star*. Little did I know that this launched my next phase as an arts and agricultural advocate.

board. Like most of my introductory work with other nonprofits, I started by organizing events with other interesting and involved volunteers, and then progressed into leadership positions, first on committees and then within the larger organization.

The museum had experienced disruptive turnover in leadership since 2012, and as a result was in serious financial trouble. In 2016, I went to work as development director in an attempt to help save the cash-strapped institution. I did some good work, but was most effective working in tandem with Elena Brokaw. Elena, now executive director of the museum, is the person who truly has saved this important repository of county history and art.

Although I think I have accomplished a great deal with the many nonprofits I have worked for or volunteered with, the real benefit has been personal. The most important result of what I have done is the wonderful people I have met and the many friendships I have made during these years.

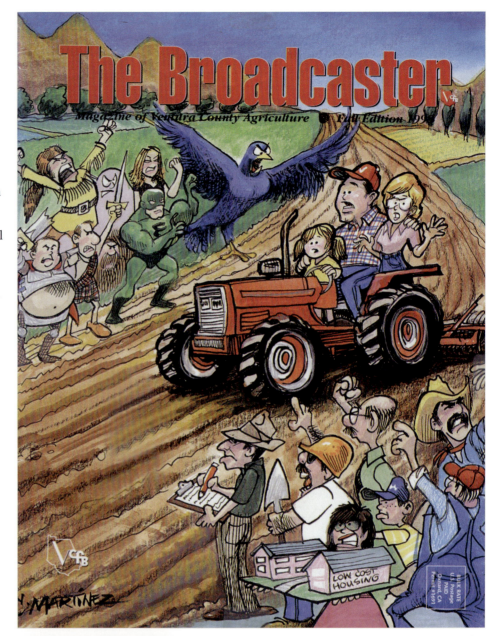

Fall 1998 edition of the *Broadcaster Magazine,* which I edited and published from 1988-2013. Artist Chris Martinez created this satirical look at farmers caught in the middle of competing forces involved in SOAR (Save Open Space and Agricultural Resources) in 1995.

Here I am in 1993 in front of a broadcaster, a machine which broadcasted both seed and fertilizer. The agricultural connection to the word "broadcaster" was fading, so I changed the name of the magazine to *Central Coast Farm & Ranch* in 2004.

Full Circle

ALSO IN 2016, AN OPPORTUNITY occurred I never would have thought possible. My brother John retired and I was elected to join the board of directors of the Limoneira Company, the first women to sit on the board since 1974, and only the third woman to be on the board in the company's 125-year history.

I remember sitting in a room full of men as I was being interviewed for the position. I was pleased the way the interview had gone, but I also appreciated the irony of being considered for a job as much for my family connections as for my personal accomplishments. There was a pause and I looked around the room and said, "Gentlemen, it's time." I was proud to be challenging the status quo in the name of all the strong women in my family who had gone before me.

Limoneira has always been generous, but the task of allocating charitable donations was rather ad hoc and was becoming more difficult and time-consuming as the number of requests increased. The board created a philanthropy committee to manage its giving and appointed me chairperson. Helming that committee has proved to be a perfect fit—a chance to employ my expertise in nonprofit management for the benefit of a company that has meant so much to me and to the community.

Dick and I in 2005 at a Ventura Music Festival event at Old Creek Winery in Ojai.

I remember thinking as I joined my first board meeting in January 2017, that I had trained my whole professional life to sit in that seat. The learning curve has been steep, but with my varied experience writing about agriculture, I was grateful that I at least spoke the language.

Dick Chess, his family and my own supportive family have been with me every step of the way and I am so heartened by their continued presence in my life, especially since we lost Dick in December 2013.

Much as I have missed Dick, I am glad he wasn't here to witness the devastation when the Thomas Fire roared into Ventura on the night of December 4, 2017, destroying more than 550 homes in Ventura and Santa Barbara—which included thirty-six homes lost in our own neighborhood. I evacuated to my brother John's home in Camarillo with my animals and a few personal items. Thankfully, although much was damaged, my home was saved. A month later, Santa Barbara was again devastated when a mudslide caused by rain on fire-ravaged hillsides swept through Montecito, killing twenty-three people.

I also appreciate another great irony and huge blessing. All of the source books I have used in writing this memoir and all of the wonderful photos that you now enjoy, would have been lost had my home been destroyed that night.

My home, surrounded by flames, at 1AM of December 5th. I had evacuated an hour before, but an intrepid neighbor captured this shot.

Workman repairing windows in my home. Every door and window had to be replaced.

The smoldering remains of the palm trees and other landscaping that burned within 20 feet of my front door.

The fire burned a beautiful tree that grew before a wall not far from my front door. It presented a blank canvass that I decided to fill with a mural. Ryan Carr, then artist in residence at the Museum of Ventura County, created sketches of a phoenix. I loved this one, but thought it too "goose like"— a phoenix needed to look proud and fierce!

ABOVE: The completed mural was just what I envisioned—a proud phoenix arising from the ashes of the Thomas Fire with the Ventura coastline I see from my home as a backdrop.

Inset (above): a copy of the letter to the editor I sent to the *Ventura County Star* at the end of July 2020, in the wake of the dismantling of the Father Serra statue in front of Ventura City Hall.

Ryan and me with the finished artwork.

The last portrait of all of us together taken at Thanksgiving 2007 by my step-sister Angela Neal Grove. Jim is on the left, mom in the middle, flanked by John and me.

The family at the Saticoy Country Club in 2006. L to R seated: Elizabeth, John, Betsy, Kai (John's wife) Standing L to R: Devon, Vince and Dick.

Me as Glinda the Good at a Rotary Club of Ventura party. Yes, I can be silly!

Afterword

IF YOU ARE STILL HERE READING THIS, thank you.

I'd like to conclude with a few thoughts about the changing role of agriculture today and how it affects virtually every aspect of life in Ventura County...

Water

Right from the earliest days of farming, water has been an issue. In some places there was water in abundance, such as on the Oxnard Plain where the water table in the early years of the nineteenth century was so high there were artesian springs. That's why the Oxnard brothers built the sugar beet factory there. It was said it took a ton of water to produce a pound of sugar.

In the rest of the county, however, dry land farming was the norm—walnuts, wheat, barley and apricots. The advent of citrus culture at Limoneira ushered in a new era of water management. Water has become a commodity rather than a resource and growers use every available technology to make the most of every drop. Now people and crops may be in competition for water. That's not a pretty scenario as lemons and strawberries and celery can't be put on water diets and the spectre of fields being fallowed, as is already seen in the Central Valley, may here become a reality.

Labor

The makeup of agricultural labor has followed the waves of immigration into California. One has only to look at the photographs of Limoneira's early labor force to see first Chinese, then Japanese and then Latino laborers who are the mainstay of the agricultural industry today.

I grew up on the ranch in Santa Paula where employees lived in a cluster of houses on the western edge of the property. My father was *El Patron* and my mother *La Patrona*. When I rode my horse down the dusty main street, people would come out to stare. It was a semi-feudal world I just took for granted.

For many years most agricultural employers provided employee housing that was very similar. That practice began to change in the early 1980s as more and more ranch operations discontinued employee housing partly due to a Workers' Compensation law known as the "Bunkhouse Rule." It stated that employers were liable for resident employees 24/7, not just when they were working. As a result, many farmers phased out employee housing. Limoneira is not the only ranch in the county to provide farm worker housing, but it also rents housing to farmworkers not employed at Limoneira. It currently provides more farm worker housing than any other farming company in the county.[58]

Today about 43,000 people work in Ventura County agriculture, at least fifty per cent of whom are undocumented. According to John Krist, CEO of the Farm Bureau of Ventura County, "That percentage has been dropping as more and more workers retire or head back to Mexico without being replaced by newcomers, hence the dramatic growth in the use of H-2A workers."

There is woefully inadequate worker housing available and since the advent of the current national administration, many fewer workers as well. One answer is to bring in workers on H-2A Visas. This is a program authorized by Congress whereby agricultural employers can contract with workers in Mexico and other countries to come to work in the U.S. for a specific period of time on a limited visa. Housing for the workers is strictly regulated and the expense involved means only the largest growers can participate.

This emphasis on proper housing is a residual of the Bracero Program, which ran from 1942-1964. The program was an agreement between the United States and Mexico to alleviate war-time shortages

[58] Conversation with John Krist, June 2020.

of agricultural labor. The agreement guaranteed safe and sanitary living conditions, a minimum wage of 30 cents an hour, part of which was put in a savings account in Mexico, and exemption from U.S. military service.

The agreement was extended with the Migrant Labor Agreement of 1951. The Bracero Program faced headwinds in both Mexico and in the United States due in part to practices that circumvented housing and salary rules, and was terminated in 1964.

The vacuum left by the end of the Bracero Program partly gave rise to the United Farm Workers led by Caesar Chavez and Dolores Huerta. It started in Delano in the Central Valley in the early '60s and moved into Ventura County a decade-and-a-half later.

Al Guilin, former executive vice president of Limoneira, gave this remarkable description of the labor situation at the time:

> The Bracero Program ended in 1964 creating labor turmoil in California Ag. I was hired [in 1966] by Bill Craig [Limoneira general manager] to help provide labor stability. Labor was in chaos, we hired anyone we could, many undocumented. We provided many "Letters of Employment," which allowed people to obtain Green Cards. We even had youth crews in the summer. Many of those people eventually brought their families and are still members of the community. During the turmoil the UFW used the confusions to establish a hold in the Central Valley. Their success there spilled over to the coast and eventually to Limoneira. The curious thing was that the company already had a compensation/benefit program that was better than the Union's. We had voluntary Unemployment Insurance, a medical plan, holidays, vacation, etc., and even a Credit Union. Yet we were overwhelmed with Union fervor and unable to overcome perceived or

actual problems in agriculture. Our notion was to cooperate with the Union to continue the work. In my opinion Cesar Chavez was a great organizer, a humble, spiritual and good person and did a lot of good. But his staff were lousy administrators and the local reps were unqualified and were more interested in correcting past sins than working to make the company and workers successful. The workers eventually recognized this and voted the union out.[59]

In 1978 Limoneira workers did, in fact, vote to join the United Farm Workers on a three-year contract that was then renewed for another three-year term. In 1985, however, workers voted to de-certify the union and there has been no UFW presence at Limoneira since then.

Farm workers today help to provide our food in the best and, as we are now experiencing, the worst of times. We must do a better job of bringing into the country and housing these valuable workers who contribute so much to our economy.

Land Use

In 1995, the Save Open Space and Agricultural Resources movement began and, by 2000, had swept the county. I understand the desire to save the agricultural landscape, but people must be aware that farming is far from being a static business and land use decisions must be based on economic reality. I remember driving down Hwy. 126 in the 1960s with the car windows wide open so I could smell the orange blossoms. Most of those orchards of Valencia oranges are gone now because the variety, largely used for juice, is no longer profitable to grow.

---

[59] Conversation with Alfonso Guilin, June 2020.

We farm here, but on a global scale. The "eat local" movement is admirable, however we can supply all of Ventura County's strawberry needs, for instance, on just forty-nine acres—but we supply the world, not just ourselves.[60]

Farmers do their business out in the open for all to see and many to criticize. How many other businesses are subject to that kind of scrutiny? Farmers try their best to farm wisely and safely, but must be allowed to farm and water and apply pesticides judiciously and make noise with their tractors if they are expected to stay in business.

Right now we are facing a potential threat that could be the death knell of citrus orchards in the county, not just commercial orchards, but our beloved backyard fruit trees as well. The Asian Citrus Psyllid is a tiny pest that carries the HLB disease that could devastate our industry. It arrived less than a decade ago in Florida and since has destroyed almost fifty per cent of the state's orange production, and to date there is no remedy. I am confident one will be found, but in the meantime, there will be an increase in spraying in order to control the insects. No one wants more spraying, but if we want to protect our "viewspace" to say nothing of the industry, we must.

WE ARE ALL SO INTERCONNECTED. Our experience with the Covid-19 Lockdown and the economic havoc it is creating only underscores the point. Like every other business, Limoneira is being hard hit. With seventy per cent of our lemons going to service restaurants and bars, we are being hammered. The good news is that consumers are buying more fresh fruit. And thank goodness for avocado toast and guacamole because Limoneira has large orchards of avocados as well as lemons. These sales are helping to somewhat offset the losses.

But I know Limoneira and the rest of the agricultural industry will find solutions. We will persevere. We owe it to the spirit of our founders, those risk takers and problem solvers, to do so.

---

[60] Conversation with John Krist, June 2020.

Epilogue

I CONCLUDE MY MEMOIR at a very unsettling time in our nation's history. The Covid-19 epidemic has, at this writing, killed 500,000 people in the United States, crushed the economy and torn apart people's lives. In addition, the long-festering issue of racial inequality has violently erupted and exposed deep fissures in American society. On January 6, 2021, a ragtag mob of Trump supporters stormed the capitol and sent members of both houses of Congress into hiding.

But I am an optimist and I have reasons to be. The January 20th inauguration of President Joe Biden gives me hope that America can emerge from the shadow of the past four years and strive to embody the American ideals of truth and equality both at home and around the world. Also my daughter, Devon and her husband Vince, have just had a baby girl, Eliza Joy, a sixth-generation Santa Paulan. I want Eliza to grow up in a healthy and equitable country. I want to teach her to ride a pony and send her off to school without a mask and be among children of all backgrounds and with them, face the future fearlessly. Is there still an American Dream to be had? I fervently believe there is.

Devon and Vince Cichoski with Eliza Joy.

The Southern Pacific Depot in Santa Paula welcomed the first train in 1887 and created the ability to ship fresh citrus to the East Coast. *Postcard courtesy John Nichols.*

The Santa Paula Depot today houses the Santa Paula Chamber of Commerce. *Photo by the author.*

The Blanchard & Bradley Flour Mill, built in 1874. *Photo courtesy Limoneira Archives.*

The old mill wheel resides today next to a modern building in Mill Park. *Photo by John Nichols.*

The Santa Paula Hardware Store became the Union Oil Building in 1890.

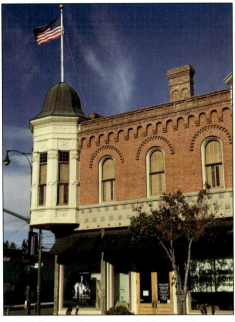

The Union Oil building today houses the Santa Paula Oil Museum. *Photo by the author.*

The Santa Paula Presbyterian Church was designed by architect Roy Wilson, Sr. in 1933. The original church was destroyed by fire. *Photo courtesy John Nichols.*

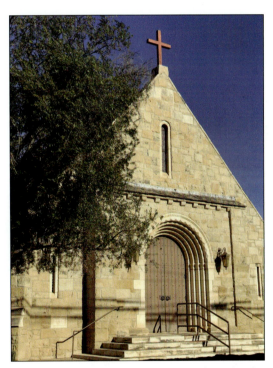

The Presbyterian Church today. *Photo by the author.*

The original Limoneira headquarters building on 10th Street/Ojai Road. *Photo courtesy John Nichols.*

The building now houses the Santa Paula Art Museum Jeanette Cole Art Center. *Photo by the author.*

The Southern Pacific Mill, after the Hengehold family purchased the business in 1954. *Photo courtesy John Nichols.*

The Mill today houses the Museum of Ventura County's Agriculture Museum. *Photo by the author.*

The Limoneira mural by artist Don Gray, 1999. One of nine in Santa Paula's Mural Project.
Courtesy Santa Paula Chamber of Commerce.

The Glen Tavern, built in 1911, was the site of Nathan Weston Blanchard Jr.'s high stakes poker games in the late 1920s. *Postcard courtesy John Nichols.*

The Glen Tavern today is still open for business with an excellent restaurant. *Photo courtesy John Nichols.*

BIBLIOGRAPHY

PRINTED SOURCES

American Families: Genealogical and Biographical from Most Authentic Sources Including Much Valuable Material Drawn from Hitherto Unpublished Family Records with Accurate Reproduction and Description of Ancient Emblazonry Compiled by Master of Genealogic and Heraldic Science... New York: American Historical Society, Inc. [1924?] "Edition de luxe limited to 50 numbered and registered volumes; no. 32."

Michael R. Belknap. "The Era of the Lemon: A History of Santa Paula, California," California Historical Society *Quarterly*, Vol. 47, No. 2 (June 1968): 113-140.

Tony Biasotti. *Limoneira Since 1893: Celebrating 125 Years of Agribusiness Success.* Santa Barbara: Pacific Coast Business Times Legacy Publication, 2018.

Dean Hobbs Blanchard. *Of California's First Citrus Empire: A Rainbow Arches from Maine to Ventura.* Edited by Grant W. Heil; drawings by Danilo Matteri. Pasadena, Calif.: Castle Press, 1963.

Nathan Weston Blanchard. *Journal* (1853-1863). The Huntington Library, San Marino, California, 1961. MssHM 91475.

Sarah Eliot Blanchard. *Memories of a Child's Early California Days.* [Los Angeles:] S.E. Blanchard. Printed by the Ward Ritchie Press, 1961.

Robert M. Clarke. *Narrative of a Native.* Los Angeles: Times-Mirror Company, 1936.

L.G. Connor. "A Brief History of the Sheep Industry in the United States." Agricultural History Society *Papers.* Vol. 1 (1921): 89, 91, 93-165, 167-197.

[Jefferson Crane] "The Narrative of Jefferson Crane: As Told to E.M. Sheridan in 1921," Ventura County Historical Society *Quarterly*, Vol. 1, No. 3 (February 1956): 12-16.

Vernon M. Freeman. *People-Land-Water: Santa Clara Valley and Oxnard Plain, Ventura County, California.* Los Angeles: Loren L. Morrison, 1968.

Mary Alice Orcutt Henderson. *The History of Santa Paula, From Metates to Macadam, Prehistoric Times to 1917.* Santa Paula: Santa Paula Historical Society, 1980.

John Krist. *Living Legacy: The Story of Ventura County Agriculture.* Ventura: Ventura County Farm Bureau, 2007.

Margo McBane. "Whitening a California Citrus Company Town: Racial Segregation Practices at the Limoneira Company and Santa Paula, 1893-1919," *Race and Ethnicity*, Vol. 4, No. 2 (Winter 2010): 211-233. Ohio University Press.

BIBLIOGRAPHY

PRINTED SOURCES

Martha Menchaca. *The Mexican Outsiders: A Community History of Marginalization and Discrimination.* Austin: University of Texas Press, 1995, 2010.

Oregon Pictorial and Biographical De Luxe Supplement. Chicago: S.J. Clarke Publishing Company, 1912.

Porter E. Sargent. *A Handbook of American Private Schools: An Annual Publication.* Boston: Porter E. Sargent, 1916.

David R. Stoeklin and Carrie Lightner. *Dude Ranches of the American West.* Ketchum, Idaho: Stoeklin Publishing and Photography, 2004.

Mitch Stone. *The Oaks of Santa Paula: A History of Santa Paula Canyon and the Oaks Neighborhood.* Santa Paula: Fern Oaks Press, 2011.

Yda Addis Storke. *A Memorial and Biographical History of the Counties of Santa Barbara, San Luis Obispo and Ventura, California, Illustrated.* Chicago: Lewis Publishing Company, 1891.

Charles Collins Teague. *Fifty Years a Rancher: The Recollections of Half a Century Devoted to the Citrus and Walnut Industries of California and to Forwarding the Cooperative Movement in Agriculture.* Los Angeles: Printed by Anderson & Ritchie: Ward Ritchie Press, 1944.

ORAL INTERVIEWS

Conversation with Alfonso Guilin, June 2020.

Conversation with John Krist, June 2020.

Conversation with John Orr, September 2020.

About the Author

Betsy Blanchard Chess

Born in Santa Paula, California, Betsy attended high school at the Bishop's School for Girls in La Jolla and did both graduate and postgraduate work at the University of Southern California, earning a Master of Arts degree in Modern European History.

Since 1988, she has pursued a dual career both as an agricultural journalist and non-profit arts manager, editing and publishing the *Central Coast Farm & Ranch* magazine while serving in top executive positions for the New West Symphony, the Rubicon Theater Company and the Museum of Ventura County.

Betsy has been recognized numerous times for her work in the arts and the community. She has earned five Paul Harris awards from the Rotary Club of Ventura; received a Woman of Vision award from the Ventura Interfaith Ministerial Association; and an Arts Star award from the Ventura County Arts Council. Additionally she was honored by Women's Economic Ventures as a

Trailblazer; chosen Ventura County Volunteer of the year by the American Society of Fundraising Professionals; and named one of "25 over 50" by the *Ventura County Star* newspaper.

In 2016, Betsy was elected to the board of the Nasdaq-listed Limoneira Company, the third woman to serve in its 128-year history and the first woman on the board since 1974.

Chess lives in Ventura, not far from her native Santa Paula, with a Portuguese Water Dog named Arrow, Cubby the barn cat, and seven backyard chickens. Betsy is an avid reader, an accomplished equestrian, a gardener and creative cook, and a musician of sorts. She is grateful to have shared her experiences in this debut book.

Daughter of the Land:
*Growing Up in the Citrus Capital
of the World:* A Memoir
by
Betsy Blanchard Chess

Printed March 2021
in an edition of
1,000 copies
Smyth-sewn
&
Hardbound

Typefaces used

Minon Pro
developed in 1990
by Robert Slimbach for
Adobe Systems
and
ITC Stone Serif
developed in 1987 by
Sumner Stone, Typographer
for the
International Typeface Corporation
and
Gill Sans
developed in 1928
by Eric Gill
for the
Monotype Drawing Office

Cover and Text Design
by
Charles N. Johnson

HISTORY *by* **DESIGN**
Ojai, Calif.

Print Production
by
Proven Print Services
Camarillo, Calif.
USA